KENK

POP SANDBOX
PRODUCTION AND PUBLISHING

Produced and Conceived by **Alex Jansen**

Written by **Richard Poplak**

Filmed and Designed by **Jason Gilmore**

Illustrated by **Nick Marinkovich**

Published by **Pop Sandbox**

Kenk: A Graphic Portrait
Produced and published by Pop Sandbox Inc.

Pop Sandbox Inc.
PO Box 16017
1260 Dundas St W
Toronto, ON
Canada M6J 3W2
www.popsandbox.com

Second edition: 2010
ISBN: 978-0-9864884-0-5
Printed in Canada

10 9 8 7 6 5 4 3 2

Library and Archives Canada Cataloguing in Publication data available upon request to the publisher

Distributed in Canada by:
Raincoast Books
9050 Shaughnessy St
Vancouver, BC V6P 6E5
Orders: 800.663.5714

The Pop Sandbox logo was created by Seth and developed from initial concepts by Jason Gilmore.

$50

Producer & Publisher's Note

All the images and dialogue in this book are taken directly from filmed video footage, recorded interviews or licensed third-party material. There are no constructions, inventions or composite characters, and edits were made only for the purposes of intelligibility and clarity.

While the principal subjects all signed the appropriate legal documentation, they were not paid for their involvement, they did not have a hand in any aspect of the book's production, and they did not vet any of the material herein.

The ideas and opinions expressed in this work do not necessarily reflect those of the creative team. The faces and names of secondary and tertiary subjects have been obscured to protect their identity.

Alex Jansen, Toronto, 2010

Author's Note

The following is a work of journalism, with a twist. Most of the content in the book is derived from more than 30 hours of digital footage taken of convicted bike thief Igor Kenk during the year leading up to his arrest. Thus, you hold in your hands a hybrid project that simultaneously takes the form of journalistic profile, documentary film and comic book.

The images have been doctored using a now-ancient technology employed by underground artists battling state-run presses in Yugoslavia during the 80s: the photocopy machine. Kenk came of age in that country during the punk-like FV movement. This style informed - and informs of - his ethos. I came to believe that this is the prism through which Kenk sees the world.

The immigrant narrative is so often an attempt to reconcile a new reality with a fraying version of home. This is the purgatory in which many of us live. With that in mind, we enter the extraordinary universe of Igor Kenk.

Richard Poplak, Toronto, 2010

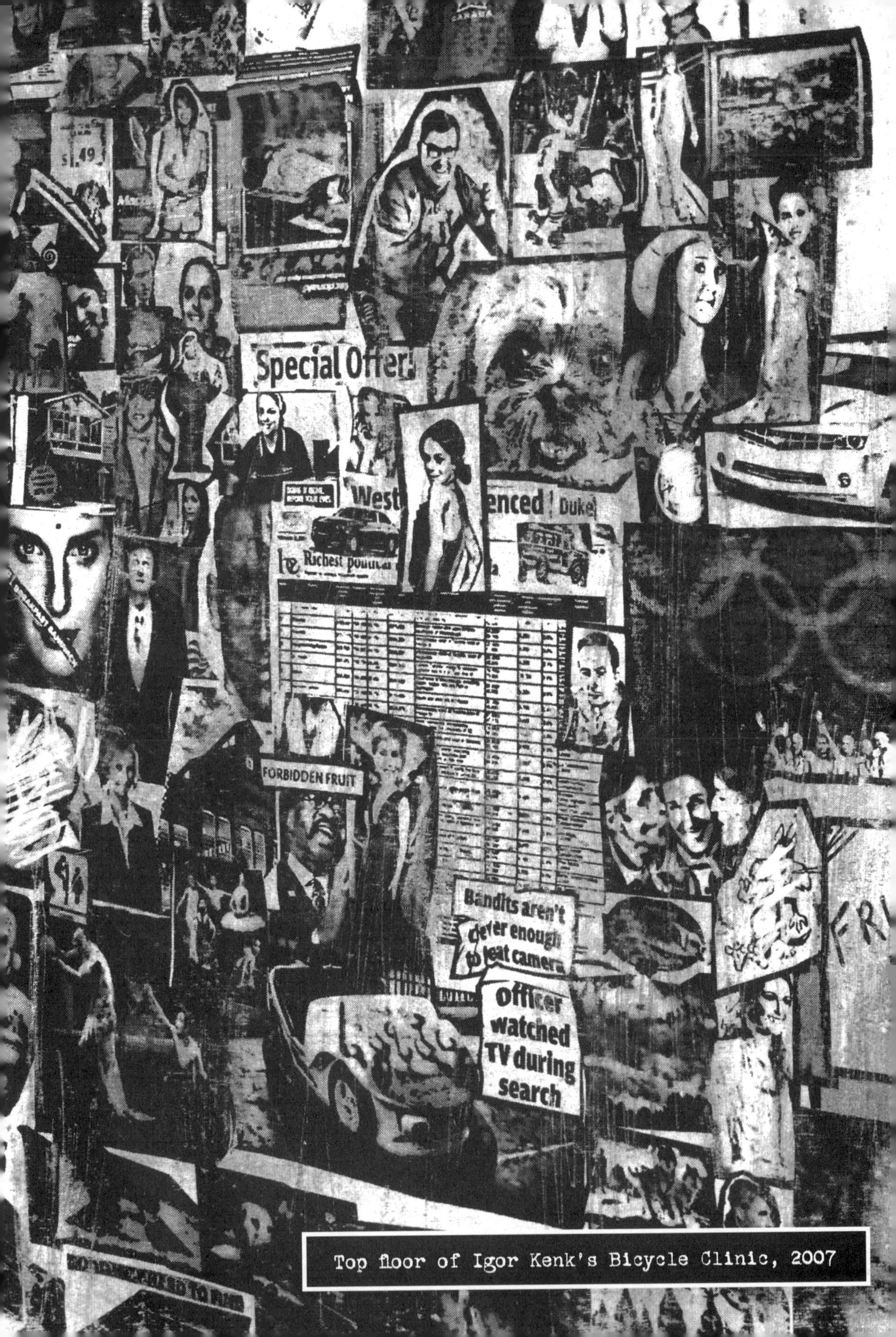
Special Offer!
FORBIDDEN FRUIT
Bandits aren't
officer watched TV during search

Top floor of Igor Kenk's Bicycle Clinic, 2007

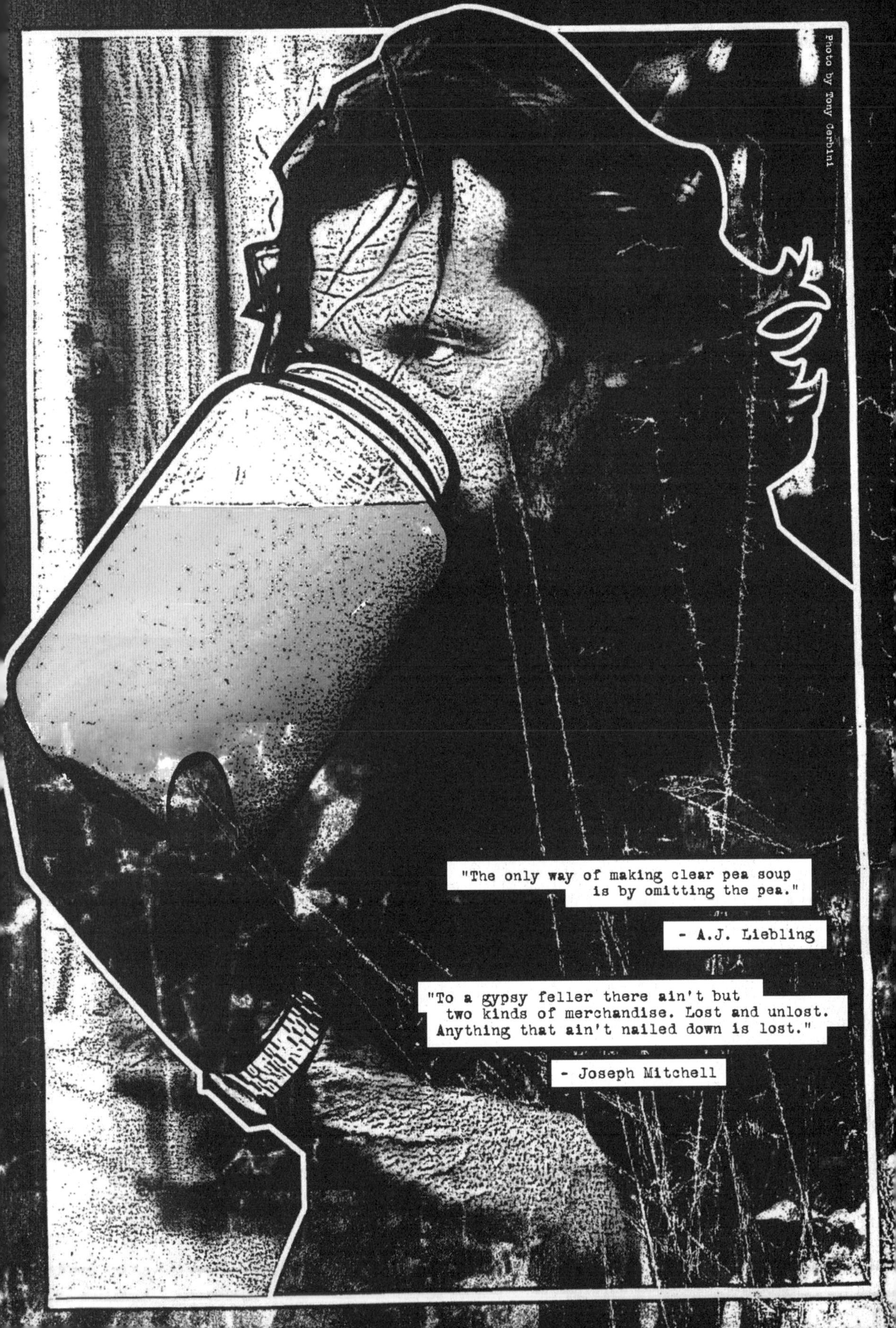

Photo by Tony Gerbini
"The only way of making clear pea soup is by omitting the pea."
- A.J. Liebling
"To a gypsy feller there ain't but two kinds of merchandise. Lost and unlost. Anything that ain't nailed down is lost."
- Joseph Mitchell

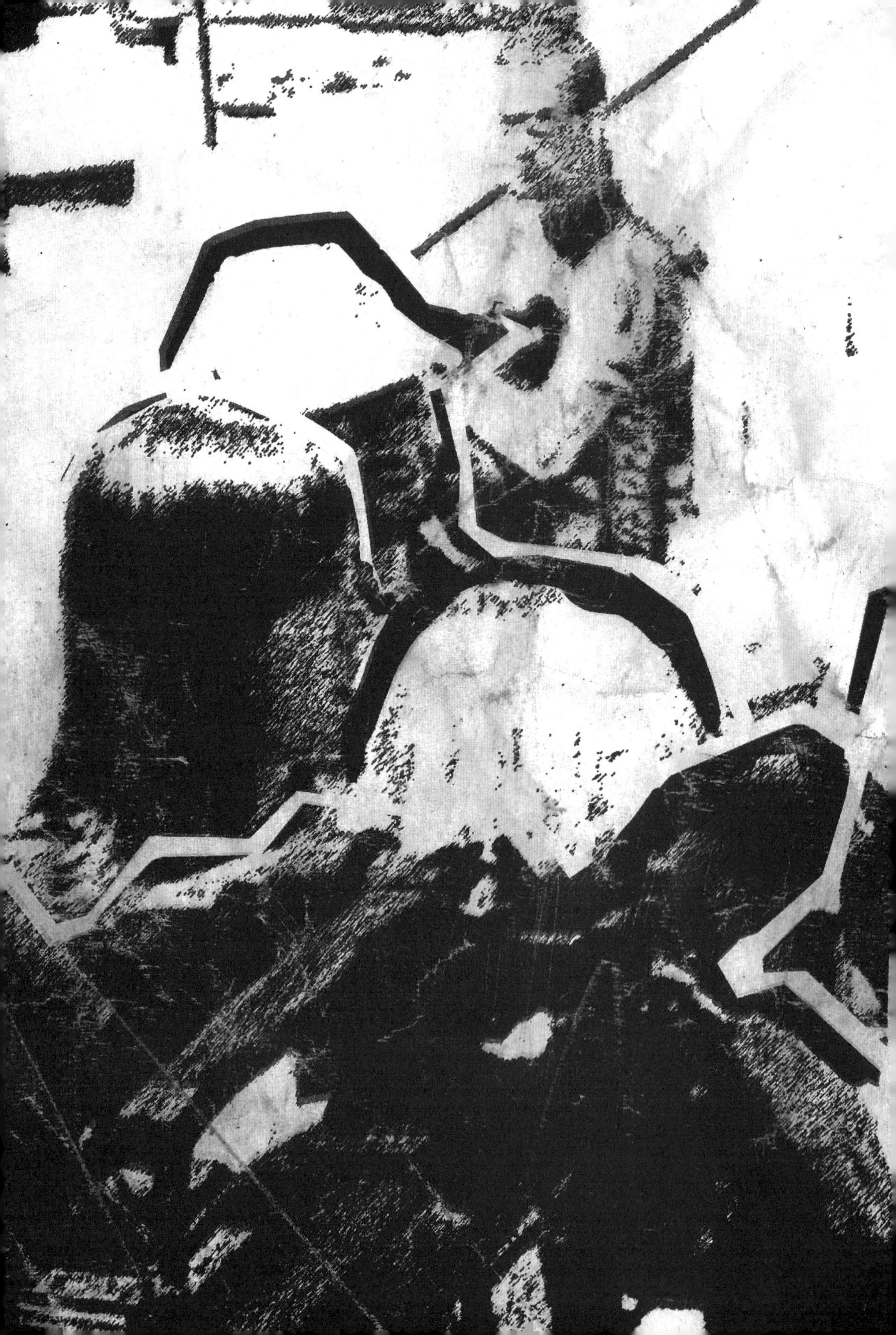

Igor Kenk's lawyer negotiates a media scrum, July 2008

PROLOGUE

July 2008
SUSPECT
IGOR KEN
"...arrested today on bicycle theft and drug charges..."
With 2,850 bicycles recovered, the question remains: What was the plan?
'A sore in the neighbourhood'
IGOR KEN
"...49-year-old slovenian-born torontonian bicycle mechanic, was taken into custody for allegedly..."
"...ordering an associate to steal a bicycle locked to a post in downtown toronto's west-end..."
"...storefront in toronto's arty queen street west neighbourhood is the centre of an alleged bicycle theft ring..."
BIKE THEFT LAIR
Home › Blogs › herb's blog
Bike Theft i
Igor = Arrested
Today is a good day!
BIKE THEFT LAIR
"...police have so far uncovered 2 additional premises, with 1,200 bicycles in various states of repair..."

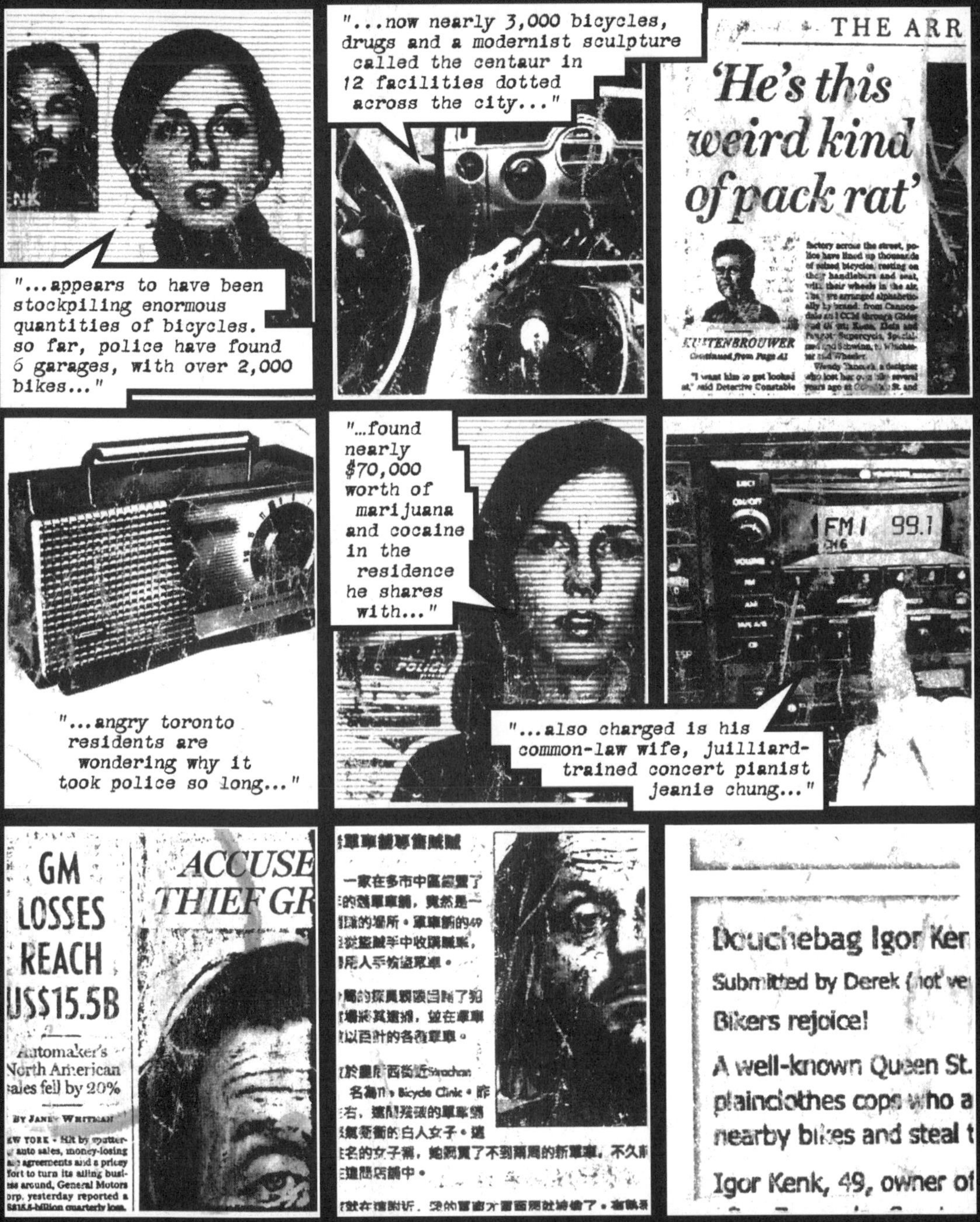
"...appears to have been stockpiling enormous quantities of bicycles. so far, police have found 6 garages, with over 2,000 bikes..."
"...now nearly 3,000 bicycles, drugs and a modernist sculpture called the centaur in 12 facilities dotted across the city..."
THE ARR
'He's this weird kind of pack rat'
KUITENBROUWER
"...angry toronto residents are wondering why it took police so long..."
"...found nearly $70,000 worth of marijuana and cocaine in the residence he shares with..."
FM1 99.1
"...also charged is his common-law wife, juilliard-trained concert pianist jeanie chung..."
GM LOSSES REACH US$15.5B
Automaker's North American sales fell by 20%
ACCUSE
THIEF GR
Douchebag Igor Ken
Submitted by Derek
Bikers rejoice!
A well-known Queen St.
plainclothes cops who a
nearby bikes and steal t
Igor Kenk, 49, owner of

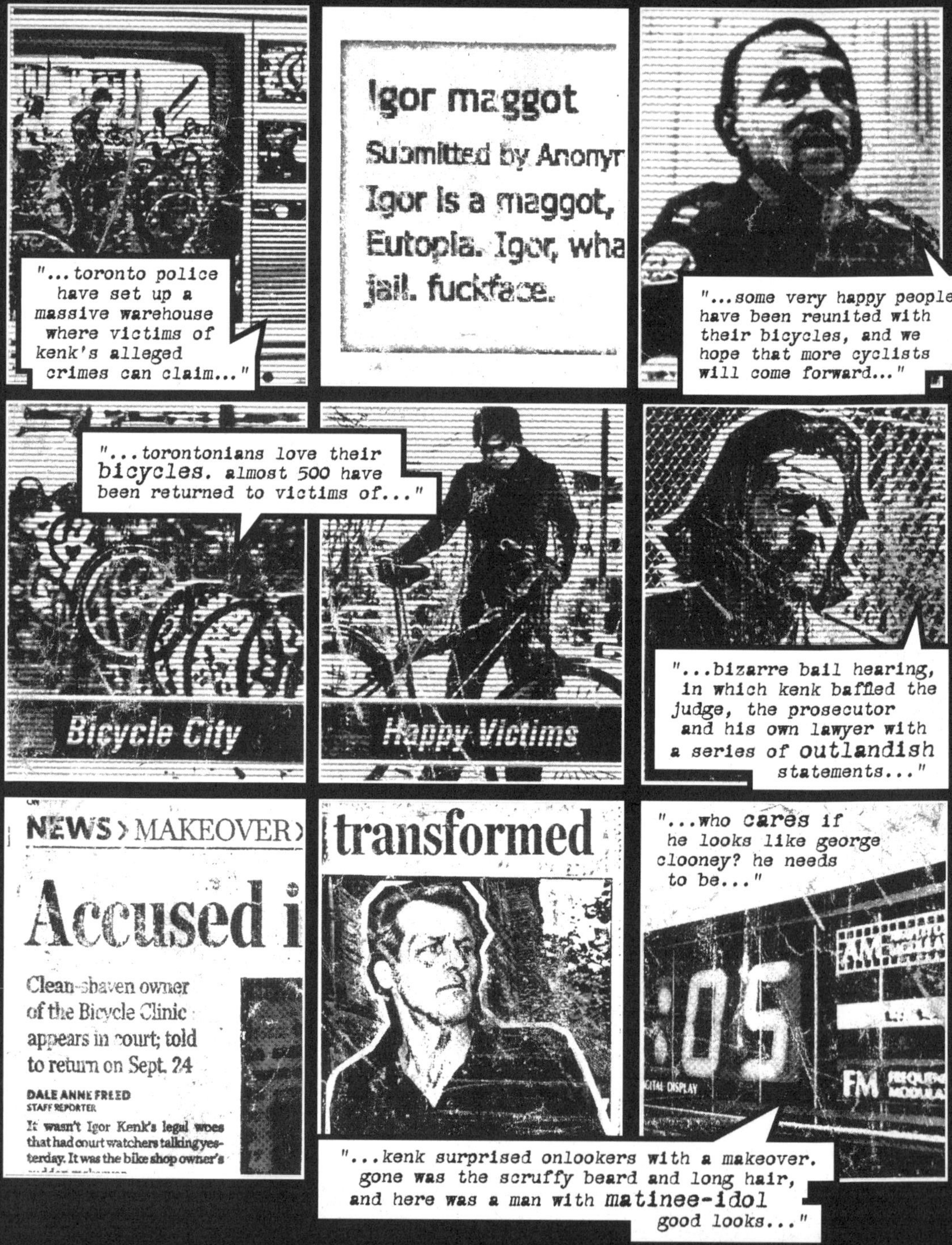
"...toronto police have set up a massive warehouse where victims of kenk's alleged crimes can claim..."
Igor maggot
Submitted by Anonyr
Igor is a maggot, Eutopia. Igor, wha jail. fuckface.
"...some very happy people have been reunited with their bicycles, and we hope that more cyclists will come forward..."
"...torontonians love their bicycles. almost 500 have been returned to victims of..."
Bicycle City
Happy Victims
"...bizarre bail hearing, in which kenk baffled the judge, the prosecutor and his own lawyer with a series of outlandish statements..."
NEWS › MAKEOVER ›
Accused i
Clean-shaven owner of the Bicycle Clinic appears in court; told to return on Sept. 24
DALE ANNE FREED
STAFF REPORTER
It wasn't Igor Kenk's legal woes that had court watchers talking yesterday. It was the bike shop owner's
transformed
"...who cares if he looks like george clooney? he needs to be..."
"...kenk surprised onlookers with a makeover. gone was the scruffy beard and long hair, and here was a man with matinee-idol good looks..."

"...despite his new, cleaned-up image, one veteran cop said..."
Kill Igor
Submitted by
http://www
OLD CITY HALL
"...that kenk was hit with the toughest bail conditions he's seen in his 25 years on the force..."
and charged with 58 offences related to bike theft and drugs.
Last week, Justice Bruce Young granted bail set at $275,000 to the then bearded, long-haired accused, ordering him to live with a surety under house arrest.
Kenk's bail was set at $250,000 for provincial charges related to bike theft, $10,000 for the federal charges including 21 drug offences, and $15,000 surety bail to be split by three supporters.
While under house arrest, Kenk won't be able to step outside unless
f his three
nk was ordered to
Die Chronik
IE BESTE FIETS SKELM
N DIE WERELD!
"...local residents rejoiced as firefighters emptied the dangerously cluttered store..."
"...and along with the international media, want to know..."
QUEEN ST. WEST, TORONTO
"...who is igor kenk..."
"...did he steal 3,000 bicycles..."
"...and what was he planning to do with them?"

PART I

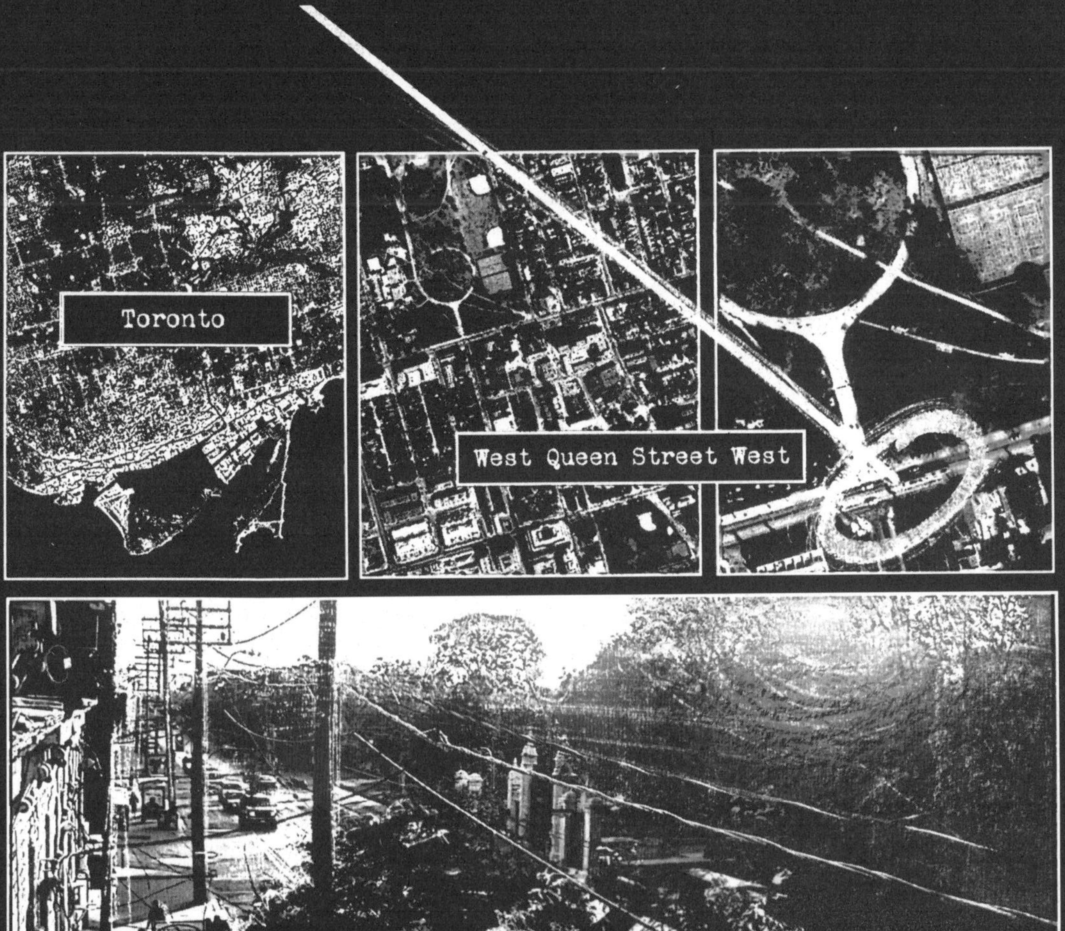
Toronto
West Queen Street West
Trinity Bellwoods Park

The Bicycle Clinic, 927 Queen West
IGOR
"I'm a villain."

927
Back in old communist shithole I was legend.
Here, I'm just a loser.
From the old shithole, they call. The first 5 to 10 years they ask me, 'Are you a gazzilionaire now?'
And I say, 'No. I'm just a pro monkey.'
Enter at Your Own Risk
Enter at Your Own Risk
And they say:
TORONTO MUNICIPAL COURT DISPOSITION
3367
927 Queen St. West
illegal breeding of Pit Bulls
Nah!

So! Public hand this shit over.
Thanks. I'll take it.
My greed factor is fuckin non-existent. I'm giving away my wonders.
North America.
We're a fat baby, sucking on milk.
We're going down.
SEVER
POLICE
TO SERVE & PROTECT
I
IM
IM TIRED
But I'm the problem, right?
I'm the worst villain in western hemisphere.

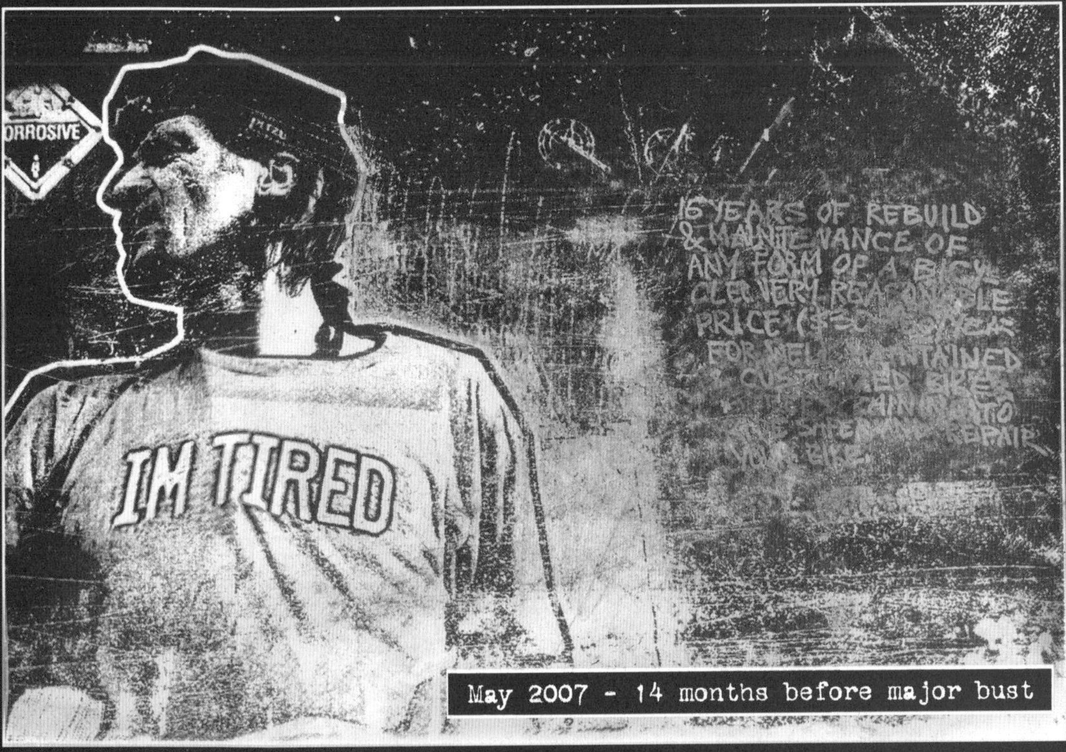
15 YEARS OF REBUILD
& MAINTENANCE OF
IM TIRED
May 2007 - 14 months before major bust

CHAPTER 1: EVERYTHING'S EASY, BABE

o-kayyy... so how much for the basket and fender?
10...12...24...35 bucks.
But we do it properly. Otherwise this things break, and it's more garbage.

Welcome to Igor Kenk's Bicycle Clinic, where the customer is NOT always right. Most summertime transactions take place on the sidewalk, which functions as Igor's outdoor workshop (for reasons that will soon become abundantly clear).

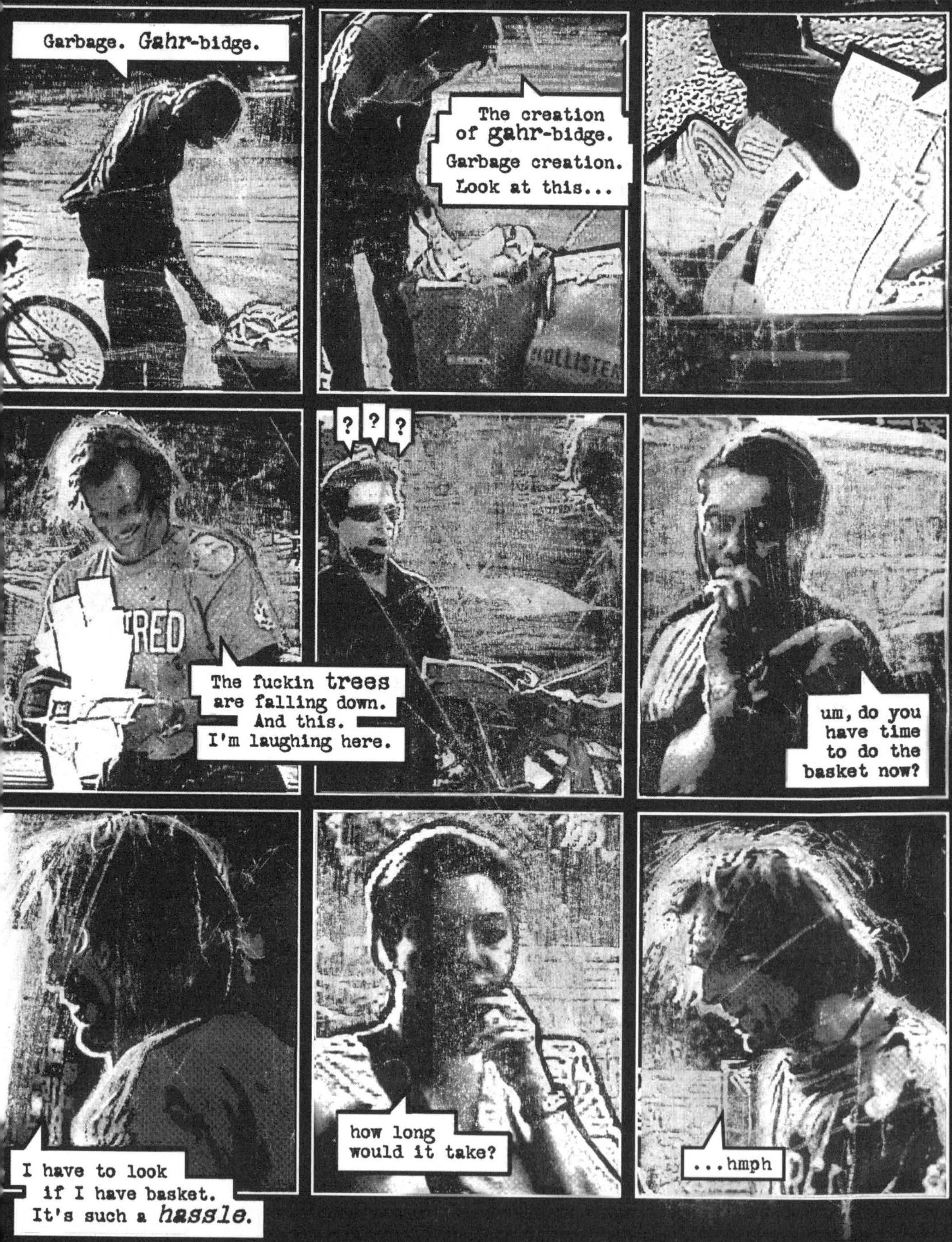
Garbage. Gahr-bidge.
The creation of gahr-bidge. Garbage creation. Look at this...
HOLLISTER
The fuckin trees are falling down. And this. I'm laughing here.
? ? ?
um, do you have time to do the basket now?
I have to look if I have basket. It's such a *hassle*.
how long would it take?
...hmph

Minutes later...
Let's peek here, you have number of options.
Oh.
Oh boy oh boy.
?
You want the rear end, babe?
um. is it easier?
Everything's easy, babe.
I'll show you.
IM TIRED
clang

After a quick rummage...

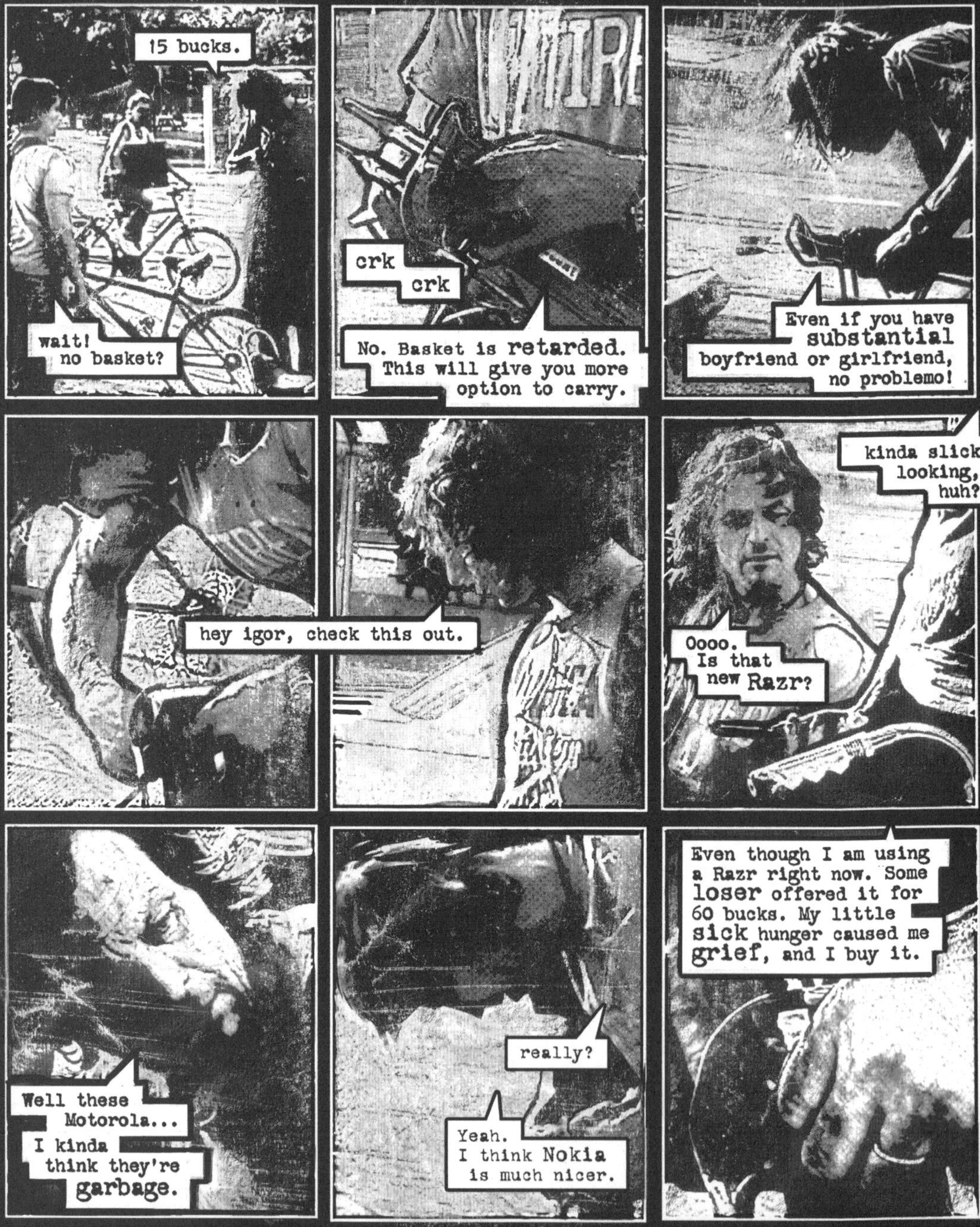
15 bucks.
wait! no basket?
crk
crk
No. Basket is retarded. This will give you more option to carry.
Even if you have substantial boyfriend or girlfriend, no problemo!
hey igor, check this out.
kinda slick looking, huh?
Oooo. Is that new Razr?
Well these Motorola...
I kinda think they're garbage.
really?
Yeah. I think Nokia is much nicer.
Even though I am using a Razr right now. Some loser offered it for 60 bucks. My little sick hunger caused me grief, and I buy it.

clang
clang
clang
♪
hullo? hullo?
um...
no signal...
shit...
brp
brp
So, needless to say, the only way you can break this fender is if you don't pay attention if it gets loose.
Things gets loose...
skin gets loose...
everything else gets loose.
um...ha ha ha!
What?
The fuck?
I say anything funny?
i hope my skin doesn't get loose.
Well, yeah, of course skin gets loose.

crk
crk
so, i can't put a basket on that?
Well, you can. But if you put a basket there, like I say, it would be retarded. You're just carrying extra weight.
but how am i supposed to carry my bag?
Just put the bungee cord on it.
hey, igor!
*
Good neighbourhood.
clink
clink

* Lech is a Polish beer that, according to the press material, "is perfect for the young on the move who do not follow the crowd and appreciate the taste of fun. Lech turns every party into an unforgettable experience. With Lech around there will be a party." Queen Street West was once mostly populated by Poles and Slovacks, who worked at the Massey Ferguson factories located south of the strip before industry left the city.

200 lbs. of weight it can carry.
Give me bag...
Okay, bungee on.
Maybe I should push one bell on you. That's a $110 fine if you don't have it.
How about one teddy bear sitting on a log?
aw. that's a good bell.
Basically, if you didn't like to look at him, you can put him upside down.
no, that's okay.
Another happy customer...
dring
dring

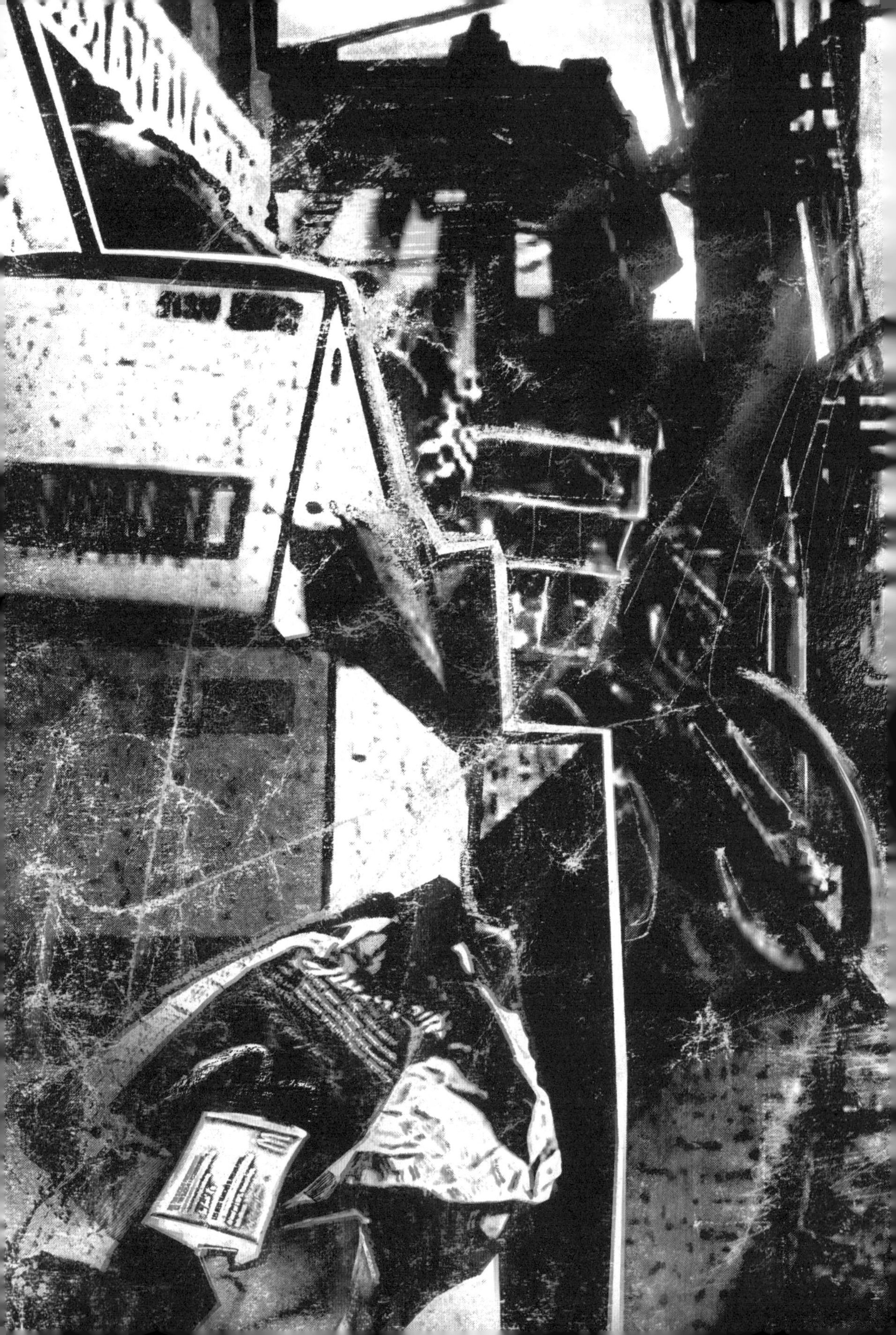

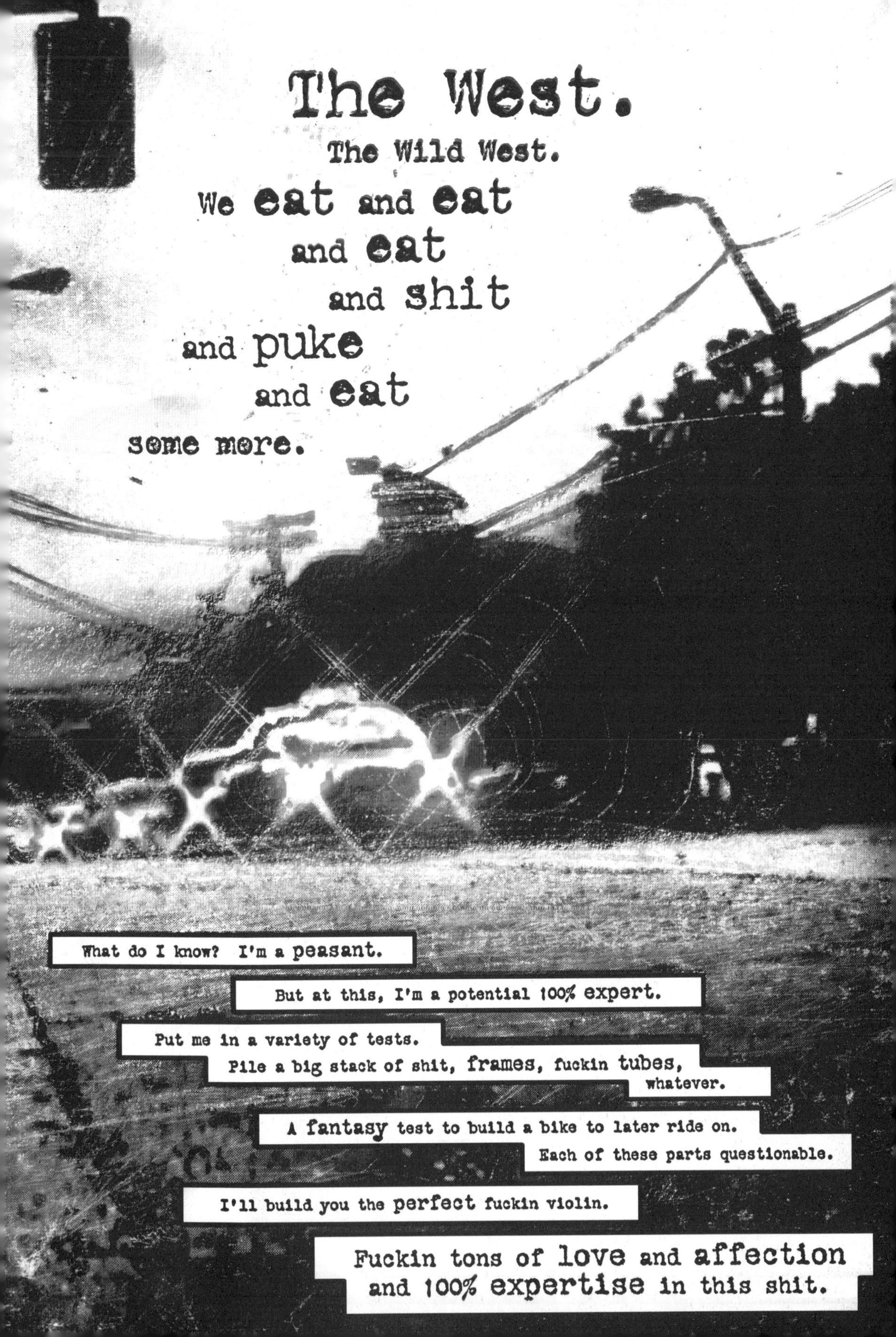
The West.
The Wild West.
We eat and eat
and eat
and shit
and puke
and eat
some more.
What do I know? I'm a peasant.
But at this, I'm a potential 100% expert.
Put me in a variety of tests.
Pile a big stack of shit, frames, fuckin tubes, whatever.
A fantasy test to build a bike to later ride on.
Each of these parts questionable.
I'll build you the perfect fuckin violin.
Fuckin tons of love and affection and 100% expertise in this shit.

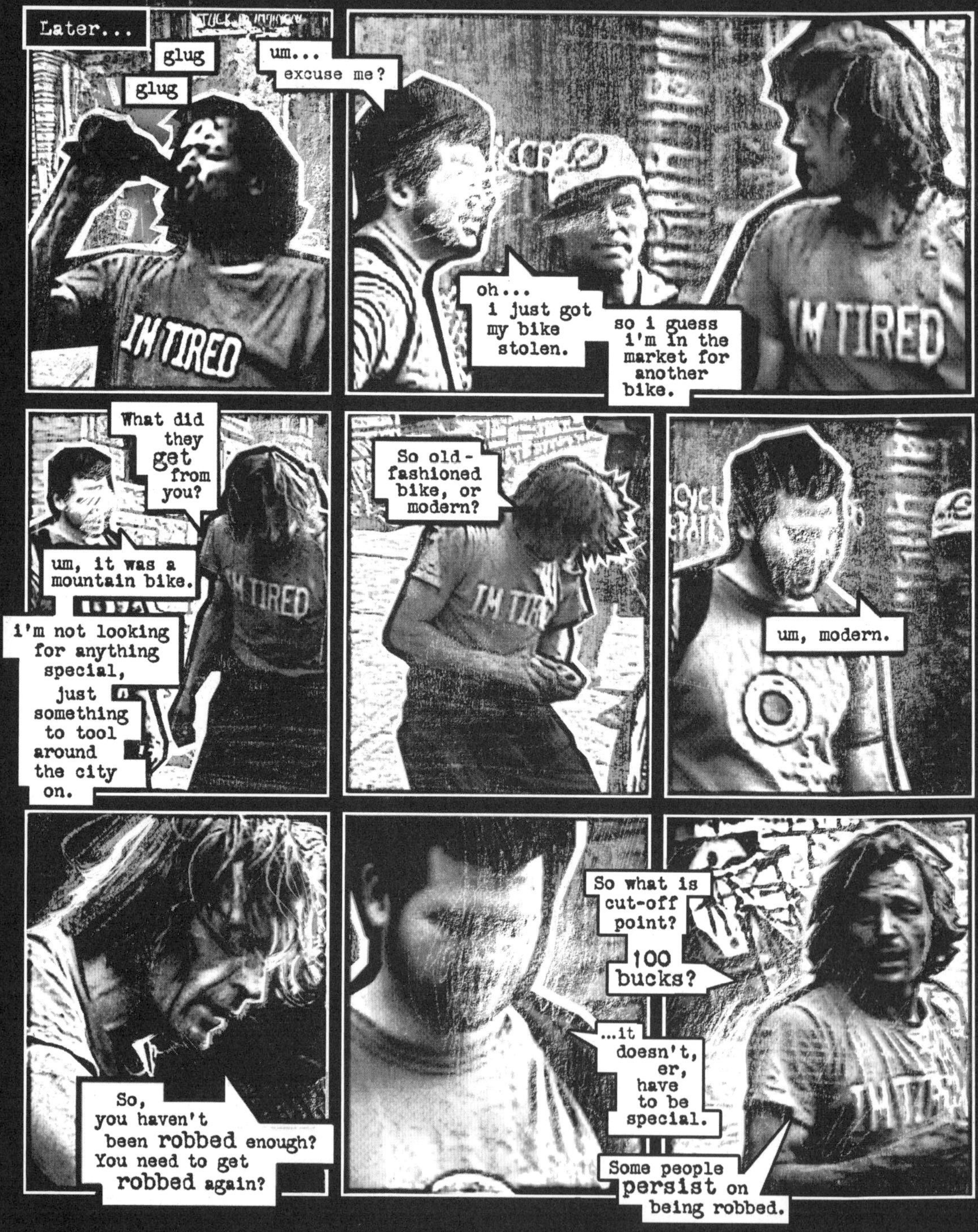
Later...
glug
glug
um... excuse me?
oh... i just got my bike stolen.
so i guess i'm in the market for another bike.
What did they get from you?
um, it was a mountain bike.
i'm not looking for anything special, just something to tool around the city on.
So old-fashioned bike, or modern?
um, modern.
So, you haven't been robbed enough? You need to get robbed again?
...it doesn't, er, have to be special.
So what is cut-off point?
100 bucks?
Some people persist on being robbed.

?
um...?
are you here tomorrow?
I'm here every day.
okay, well, i've got to be somewhere.
i'll probably be back tomorrow.
? ?
Loser.

Igor takes a break.

You see that loser? *Losers.* I can bring any piece of trash bike basically within half an hour, on the road. I can keep it for 20 bucks a year on the road, indefinitely.
But I cannot do that because the city pirates want to control me.
They want me to throw my bikes out. They call them 'junk.' So, what about the losers? What about them?
The thing is that the city, they wish to condemn the building, throw me in jail, and all this shit... *
Oh, but the lawyer is fuckin sharp man. My lawyer - he's a killer. Harry. He's disbarred.
Like he's this old Jewish guy...
He walks like a cripple...
He's probably like doing some drugs or something. He's one of these, brilliant, brilliant people who got on the wrong groove, right?
But, I hired him 3 times, and cases are just going down the drain. Toilet, man. Toilet.
I walk, the city fucks off.
Harry, though. Fucked them all up.
In 2000, they tried to take my licence away.

* Another of Kenk's endless hearings, this one a bylaw infraction for keeping bicycle scrap in his backyard. At this point, including vehicular violations, Kenk has at least 40 outstanding infractions.

Like where do they get this fuckin hillbilly city official peasants? They're no better than inmates, right?
breep
breep
Hullo? Hullo?
Dammit.
sqrk
your bikes are stolen, man! your bikes are stolen!
?
i'm just fucking with ya. i live in the neighbourhood, right?
i mean my bike did get stolen but i didn't come see you about it.
Yeah? What bike was it?

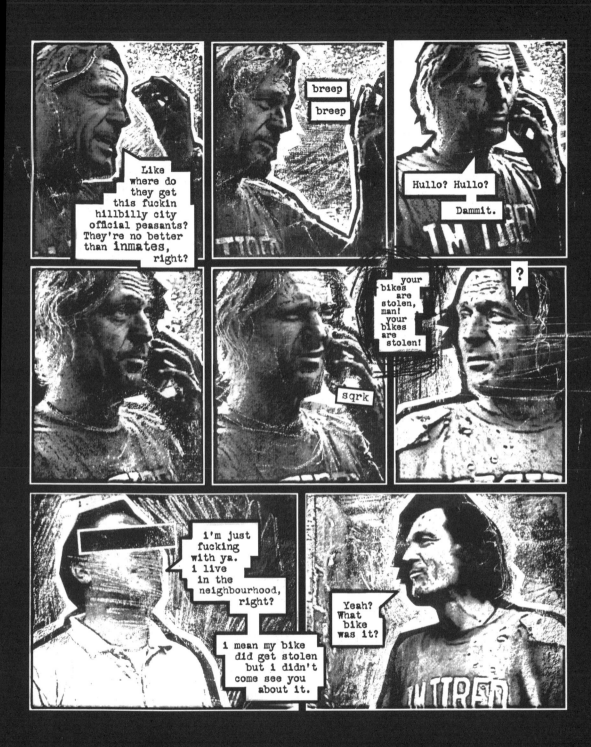

oh, it was a year ago. a long time ago.
Nice bike, or...?
yeah, it was new... but whatever.
Hmm. I must admit. I don't feel that sorry for people who have shit that's to be stolen.
what the hell does that mean?
Huh?
dude, that's bullshit!
Nooo. I, I suggest people...
Like, let's say, I bought this truck. Not new - I don't buy new...

no, no - back up. back up to what you were just saying. never mind your truck.
All I'm saying is, everybody wants to have something that looks stealable.
And I go, like, why would you want to do this? This is liability.
Especially with gorgeous women. They come and they want pretty bikes...
and I say like what fuckin for? You're just going to get robbed. There's no sense.
dude, you have no fucking argument whatsoever. that is such a bullshit excuse.
dude, I have a bike sitting in a garage downstairs.
what gives somebody the right to steal that and put it up front in your shop?
i'm listening. i'm listening...
if you ask me, you are fully involved in it. but nobody can pin it on you, so good on you.
but hey, you know what? i'd like a bike motherfuckers don't steal.
Oh yeah? Any time, man. Any time.
but if i do walk by and see my bike sitting here, then we'll have a different conversation.

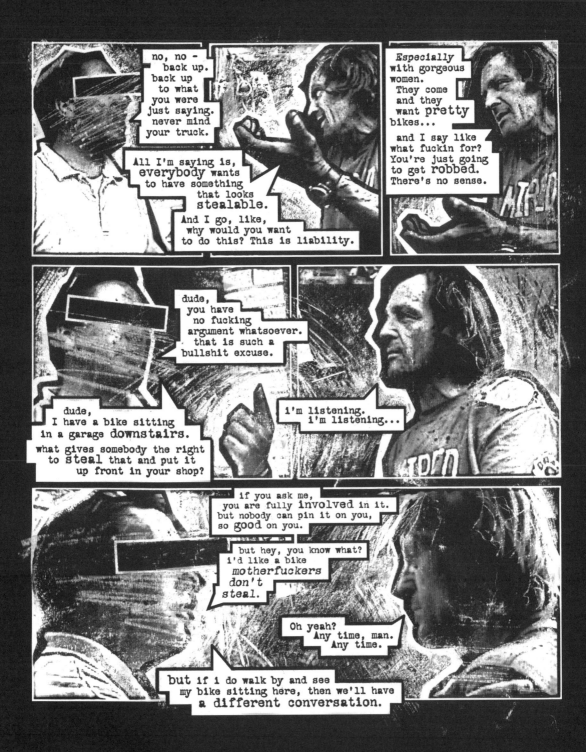

Enter at
Your Own Risk

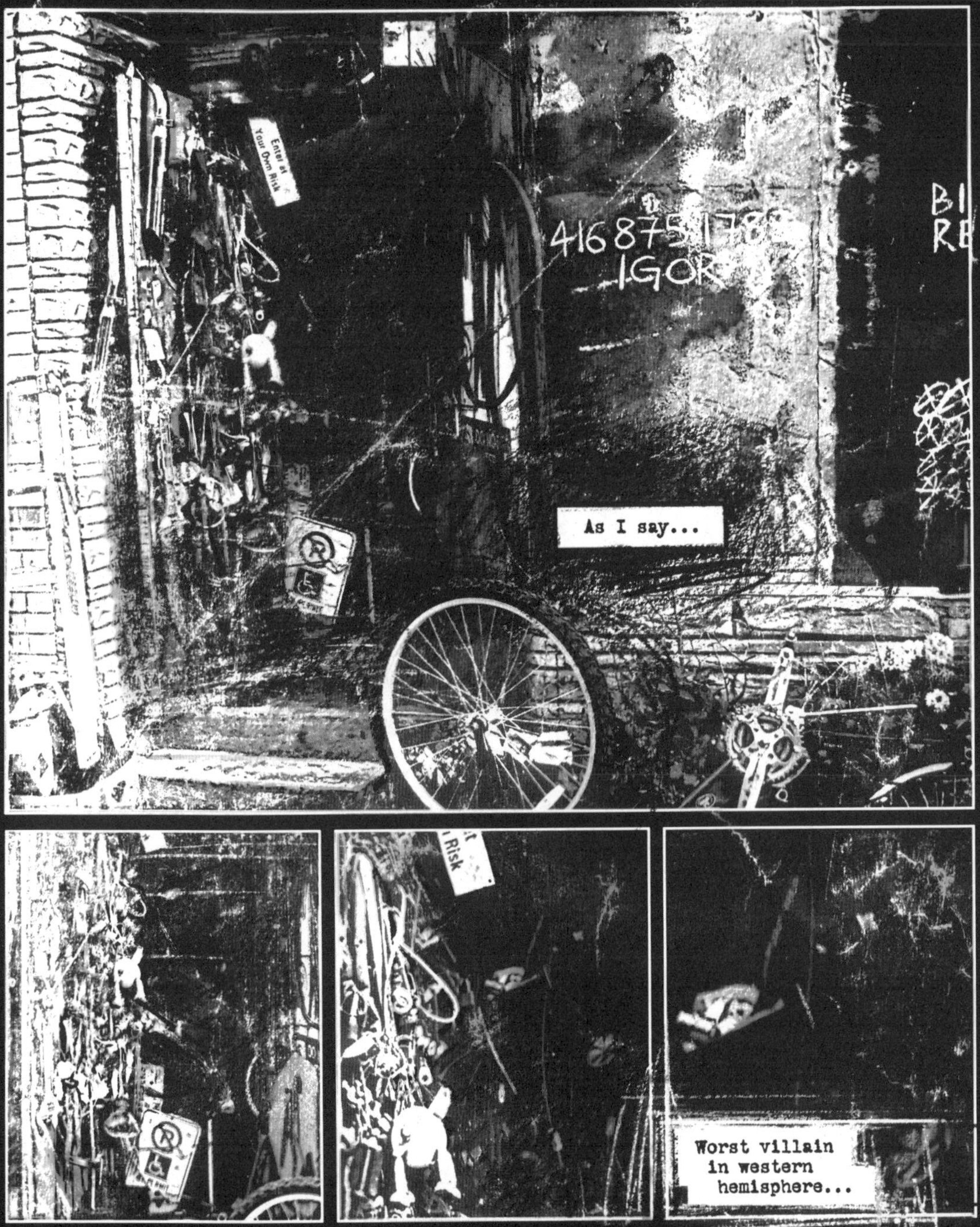
Enter at
Your Own Risk
IGOR
As I say...
Worst villain
in western
hemisphere...

IGOR'S bike clinic
BIKES OF ALL MAKES AND SIZES FOR SALE, REPAIRS
TRADE-INS, PARTS:
AFTER HOURS
QUEEN & OSSINGTON
53426 4
enviromentally responsible
very affordable.

Original Bicycle Clinic flyer, circa 1995

CHAPTER 2: MIDDLE OF ROAD MEDIUM COMMUNIST SHITHOLE

Igor Kenk, age 3, Maribor, Slovenia, 1962

I dunno. I dunno.

June 2007 - 13 months before major bust

I'm uh...
THE LAKEVIEW LUNCH
est.1947
*
I dunno.
THE
LUNCH
LLBO
est.1947
BREAKFAST
Trailblazer..............
Chuckwagon...............
Western Scramble....
TIRED

* The Lakeview Lunch, a west-Toronto greasy-spoon institution bedecked with framed images of Depression-era wrestlers, was rebranded shortly after this breakfast, as were many of the neighbouring establishments. The surrounding area, after an incredibly swift makeover, is now known as the Ossington strip. It's all become quite fancy.

igor, why don't you just order something.
anything.
*

* This is Jeanie Chung, Igor's common-law wife of 8 years. She's a Juilliard-trained pianist, one of the best in Canada. We'll learn more about her later.

Ugh...
So let's jabber - for just one second - about the old shithole...

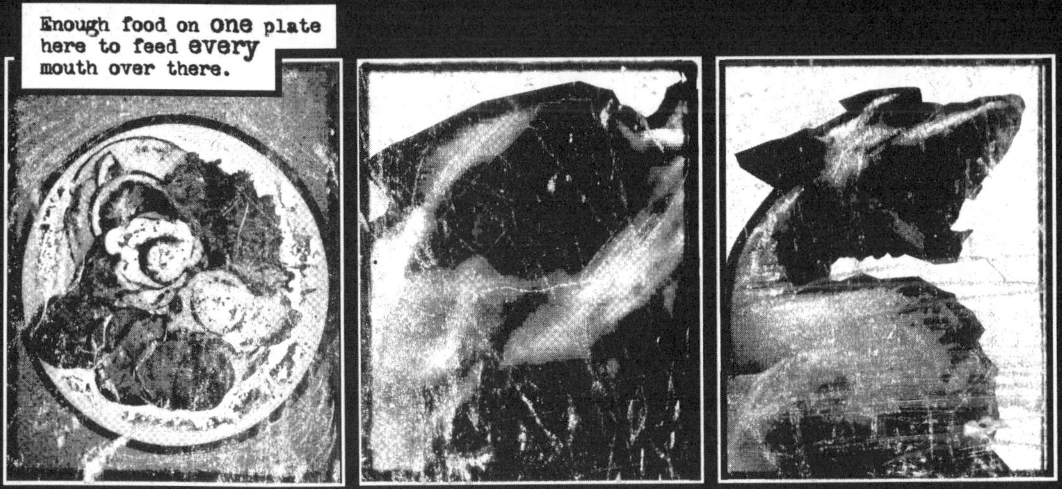
Enough food on one plate here to feed every mouth over there.

So - born Slovenia. 1959.
City of Maribor.
Under Tito's little thing.
Place was very racist,
Austria-Switzerland style.
People were fairly well behaved.
Very well educated.
But Nazi punks, basically.
Fascists.

Ljubljana, capital of Slovenia

History lesson for retards:
AUSTRIA
HUNGARY
SLOVENIA
CROATIA
BOSNIA AND HERZEGOVINA
Serbia
Montenegro
In 1945 comes to the world the great recipe of Yugoslavia.
The Great Dictator. He says fuck you Stalin, fuck you rest of world.
*
Middle of road communist shithole. No friends. Plenty of enemies.
1980. Tito was dying. It looked like it could turn into sour shit.
Which 10 years later it did.
Slovenia really fortunately got out of this crunch.
13
Yugoslavian federal troops after victory, Belgrade highway, 1991

* Josip Broz Tito, born 1892, died 1980. Architect and leader of the Socialist Federal Republic of Yugoslavia. He is perhaps the most misunderstood figure of the Cold War years - neither Stalin's stooge nor a Western puppet. Reviled as he was during his 4-decade rule, he is now credited with managing the impossible - keeping the Balkan nations from each other's throats.

A Serb soldier flashes the victory sign, Croatia, 1991

Photo by Ron Haviv

Blessedly free of the same degree of ethnic and nationalist tension as the rest of Yugoslavia, Slovenia declared independence on June 25, 1991. The remaining members of the republic descended into the horrors of the Yugoslav Wars.

RESTAURANT
sploosh
THE LAKEVIEW LUNCH
est.1947
BREAKFAST PLATES
Farm Fresh Eggs
Homemade Buiscuits & Gravy
Eggs Benedict
Hot Biscuit Sandwhiches
I'll just share whatever.
I'm not hungry.
Austria
Slovenia
LJUBLJANA
Maribor
Slovenska Bistrica
Slovenske Konjice
Rogatec
Radkersburg
Ptuj
Drava
Shit, what a life...

sonček *
Small family. One sister. Parents just low middle-class whatever. Mother a bank teller. Father a businessman dealing with small fries in agriculture.
He really fucked himself up, that guy. Genetically beautiful. Extremely good cards he came with.
But he really wasted his life away.
* *
He was gentle giant.
A nobody.
His father used to say to him, 'Idiots buy things, and smart people sell things to idiots.'
He forgot this.
I did not.

* Slovenian for "sunshine," Igor's childhood nickname
** Igor's friends in Ljubljana suggest that Igor's father had an alcohol problem. He died of cancer in 2006.

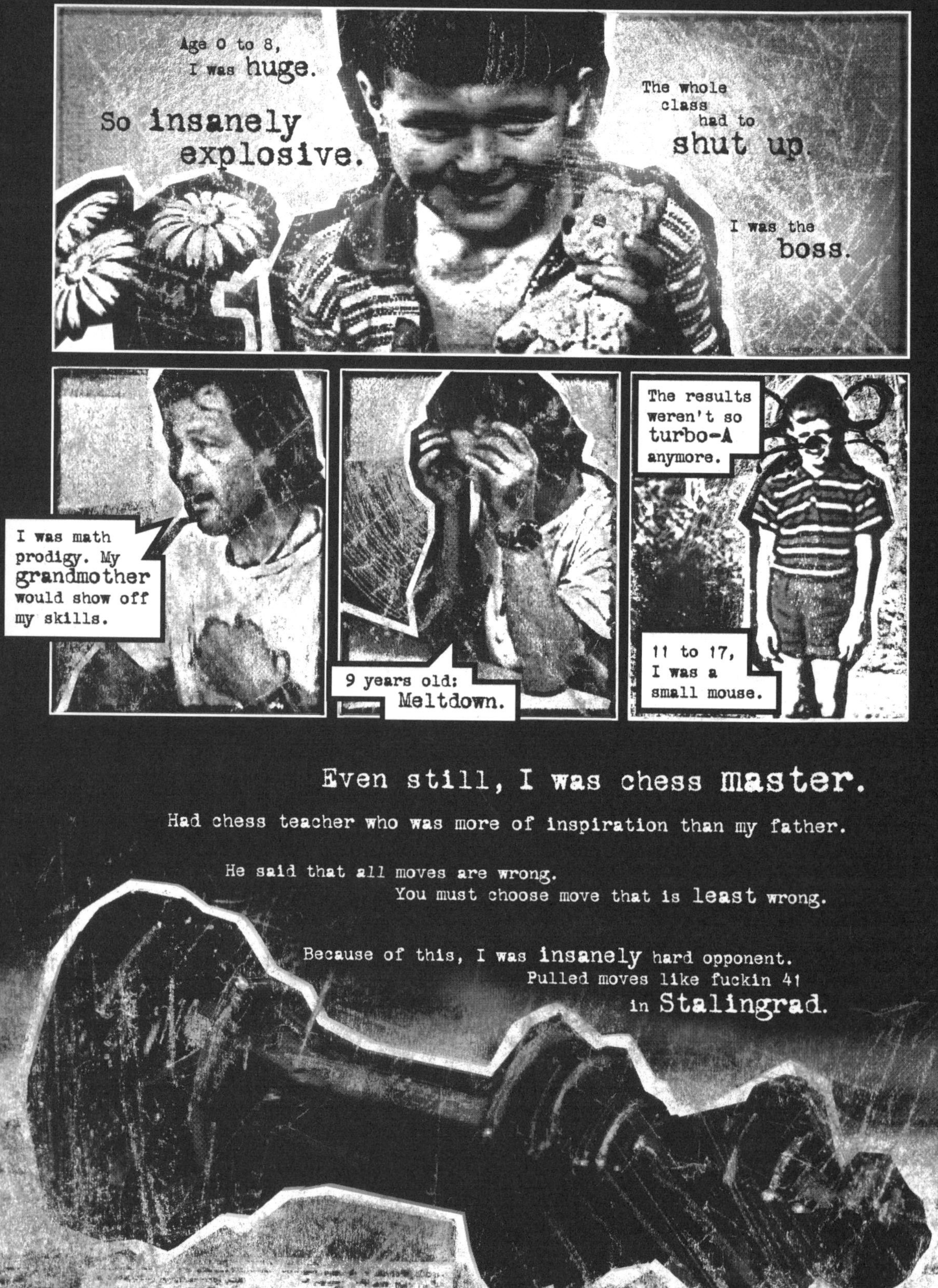
Age 0 to 8,
I was huge.
So insanely explosive.
The whole class had to shut up.
I was the boss.
I was math prodigy. My grandmother would show off my skills.
9 years old: Meltdown.
The results weren't so turbo-A anymore.
11 to 17, I was a small mouse.
Even still, I was chess master.
Had chess teacher who was more of inspiration than my father.
He said that all moves are wrong.
You must choose move that is least wrong.
Because of this, I was insanely hard opponent.
Pulled moves like fuckin 41
in Stalingrad.

It's sad, man.
Why is society not picking up on kids with driving force? It's unbelievable.
Good EQ is a better ticket than IQ. My father had high IQ. But EQ - emotional quotient - is different.
It's the drive, how much beating you can take.
kerplunk
I'M TIRED
It's crazy.
RESTAURANT
POLICE

So, I entered police academy in 74. Those police guys, of course they were funded by the state.
Every kid **wanted** to get in there, 'cause the school was considered the shit, right? I made it in there.
And they really **squeezed** the fuck out of us.
Igor Kenk, age 15, Slovenia Police Cadets, Ljubljana, 1974

Kicked us out of bed 5 in the morning. Ran 5 kilometres. Breakfast. School. Lock in. Study.
They brainwashed us. Even the guys who were clear geniuses, they fucked them up.
There were a couple of really mean personalities there.
Squeeze.
Pressed us against the wall.
Knocked the shit from us.
So, I learn how to knock the shit back.

Like in judo, right? In judo, buddy can throw you around all he wants. He's collecting points.
I'm not interested in points.

My atomic mass is too high.
My explosive power is so very high.
My biggest success was basically representation of Slovenia for cops, right? I become Slovenian Police Judo Champion. I fight a couple of stronger dudes, which one of them knocked out the other and I knocked out that one by miracle.
Like, in training he would be routinely knocking me out, but in qualifications I fuck him up. So it was great. They gave me salary plus 50%. Best.
Best.
IM TUR
Photos courtesy of Duncan Vignale, Haim Vaginshtein and Tiffany Maggio

Then, in 78, they dispatched us around the country.
Gave us fabulous salary to start with.
AUSTRIA
They put me a few kilometres from Austrian border.
It didn't work out so hot.
Igor's tenure as a policeman lasted a year. In 1980, he was almost court-martialed for making a crack about the amputation of the dying Tito's leg. Igor's mother intervened, and he was released from the force shortly thereafter.
With the death of Tito, life in Slovenia, as in the rest of the federation, hadn't been so unstable since World War II.

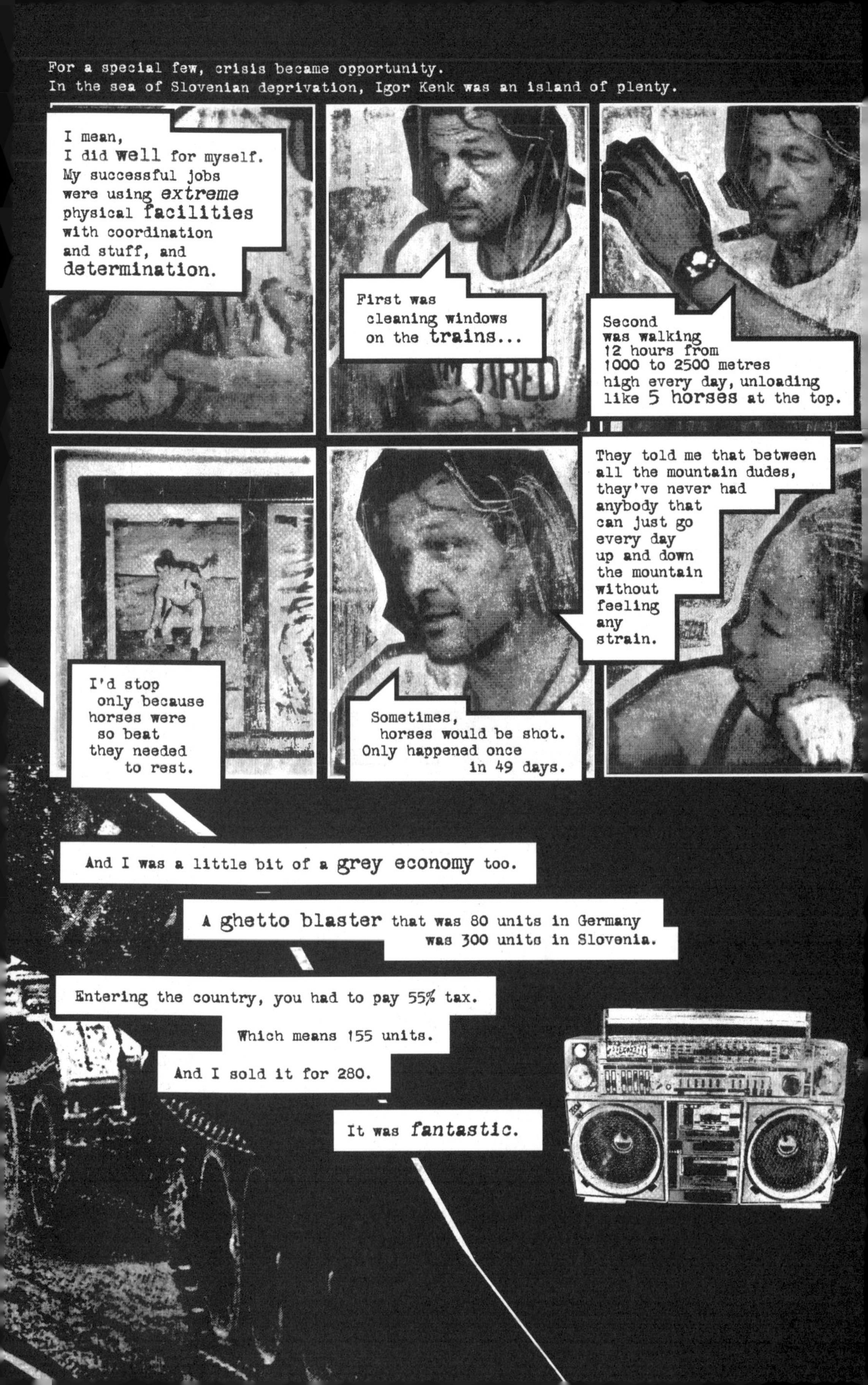
For a special few, crisis became opportunity.
In the sea of Slovenian deprivation, Igor Kenk was an island of plenty.
I mean, I did well for myself. My successful jobs were using extreme physical facilities with coordination and stuff, and determination.
First was cleaning windows on the trains...
Second was walking 12 hours from 1000 to 2500 metres high every day, unloading like 5 horses at the top.
I'd stop only because horses were so beat they needed to rest.
Sometimes, horses would be shot. Only happened once in 49 days.
They told me that between all the mountain dudes, they've never had anybody that can just go every day up and down the mountain without feeling any strain.
And I was a little bit of a grey economy too.
A ghetto blaster that was 80 units in Germany was 300 units in Slovenia.
Entering the country, you had to pay 55% tax.
Which means 155 units.
And I sold it for 280.
It was fantastic.

When the basics of everyday life became harder to come by, the ability to cross the border between Italy or Austria and Slovenia was a highly marketable skill. And Igor was a master. One of his greatest successes came from smuggling a carload of bananas into banana-starved Slovenia.

ZASTAVA
750
750 L

The game.
That's the game.
I just like to do an impossible. Back home I was legendary. Fuckin legendary.
I was icon. 'Oh ya, Igor man. The boss! Celebrity. Legend.'

Igor's status as the Banana King gave him licence to fill friends' basements with a jumble of collected stuff.

A prized possession was a gorgeous steel-frame East German racing bike - the first bike anyone remembers Igor collecting.

did you use to ride bikes back there?
Well, yeah - but not as aficionado. I was the yuppie. The ritzy yuppie. I didn't think bicycles yet - even though best fuckin invention in history of world.
Yeah - times were grand. I had one particular key babe, but she was getting considerable in the behind, and I didn't like the way this was trending.
So I dumped her.
*
So then, in 1985, I meet my dream paper wife. She gets job with Air Canada as stewardess and says, 'I wanna go study in Toronto...'
She came from ritzy parents, right? Like her mother was senior doctor, right? Her father was professor, right?
So when they saw their daughter's choice?
Yeah, so they were bugging me. How am I going to feed their daughter?
I'm thinking I'm cleaning windows, receiving 4 times per hour what you are getting combined.
So I don't understand why you people are worried about me.

* The trend may have had something to do with the "key babe's" pregnancy. In 1985 she gave birth to Igor's daughter, who currently lives in Maribor and works as a pharmacist.

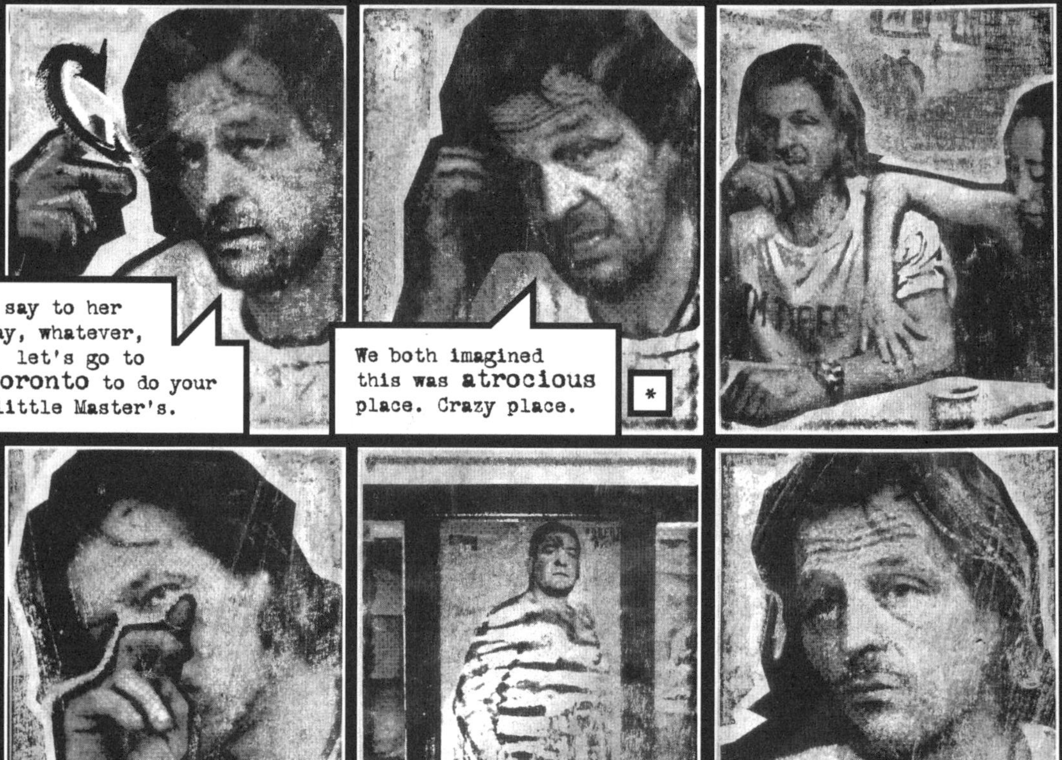

I say to her okay, whatever, let's go to Toronto to do your little Master's.
We both imagined this was atrocious place. Crazy place.
*
Toronto
What a fuckin place is this.

* This was - at best - a rocky relationship. Friends in Ljubljana recall domestic disputes that would last all night, many of them including props such as steak knives and sharp pieces of crockery. Split lips and black eyes were not uncommon.

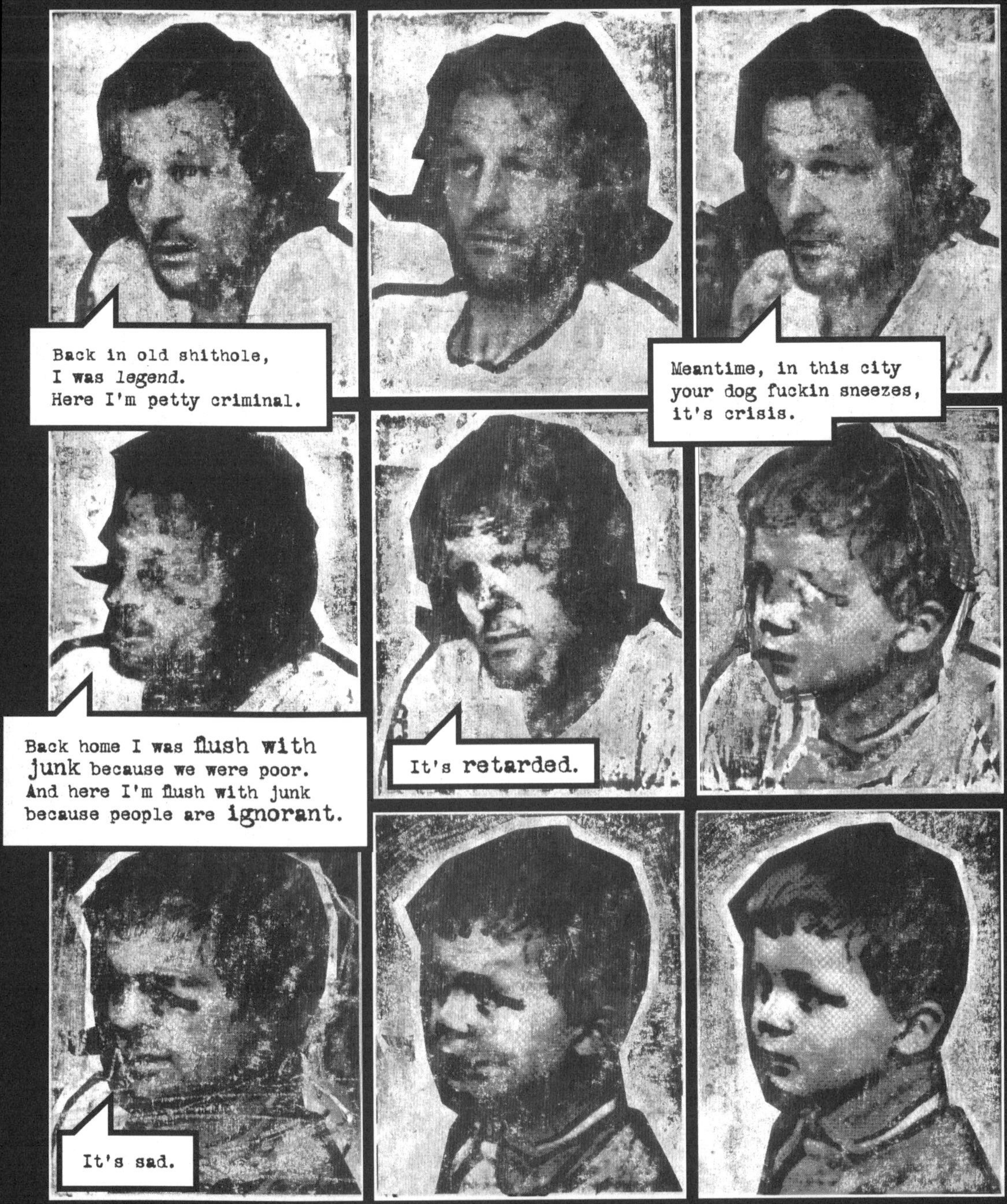
Back in old shithole,
I was *legend*.
Here I'm petty criminal.
Meantime, in this city your dog fuckin sneezes, it's crisis.
Back home I was flush with junk because we were poor. And here I'm flush with junk because people are ignorant.
It's retarded.
It's sad.

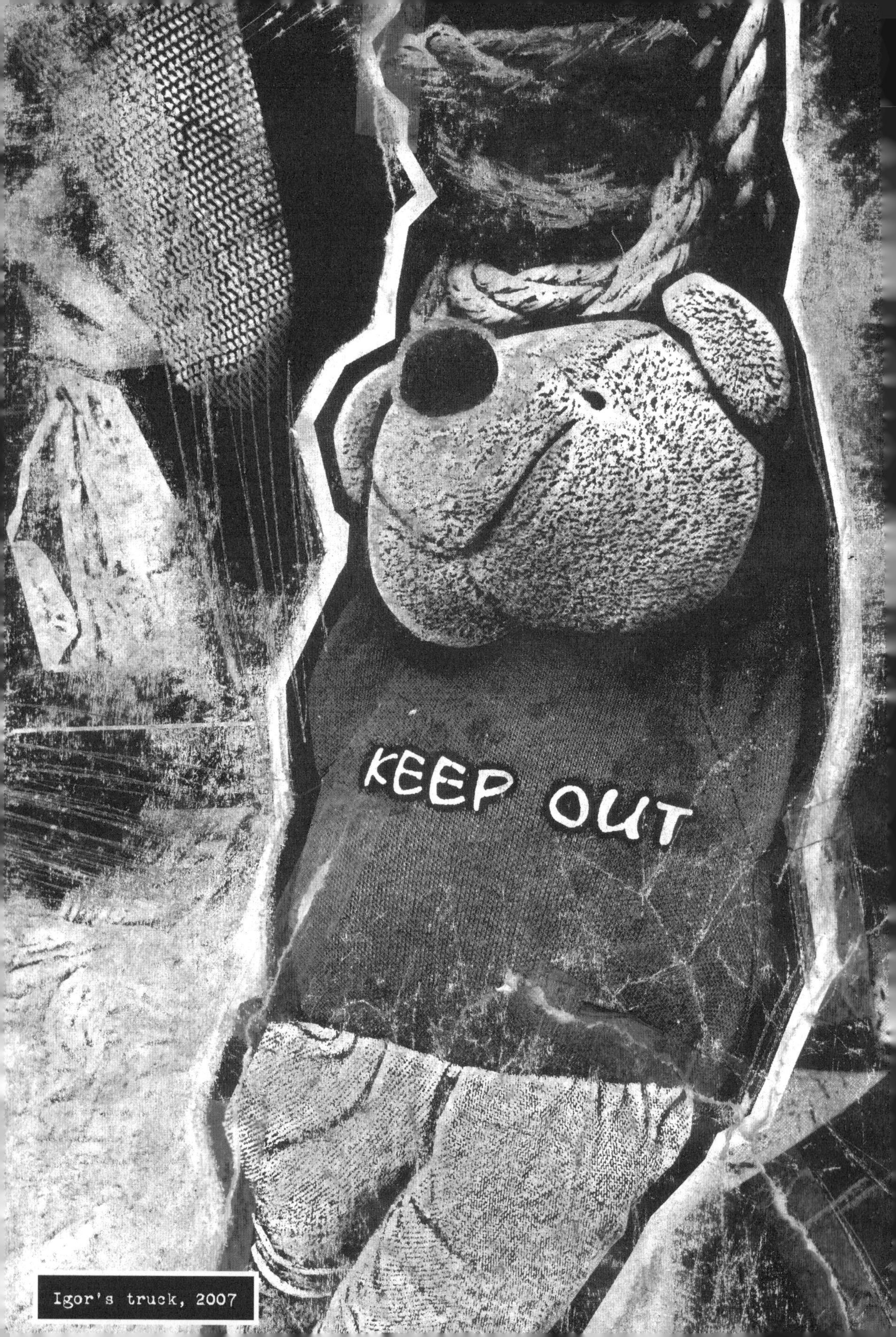
KEEP OUT

Igor's truck, 2007

CHAPTER 3: INTERESTING FUCKIN BEGINNING

Pearson International Airport's former Terminal 1 parking lot, circa 1988. The first thing most arriving immigrants saw of their new home.

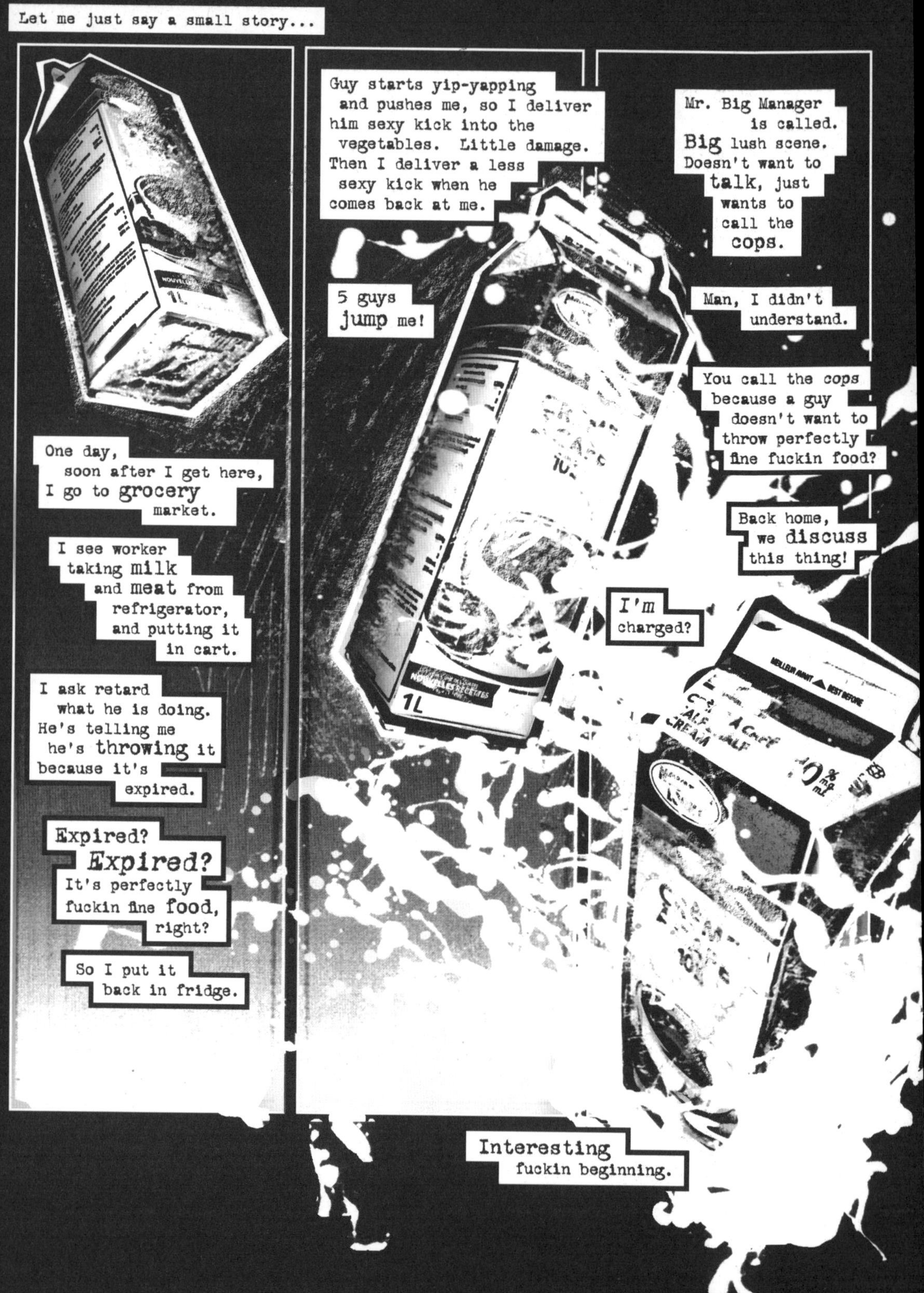
Let me just say a small story...
One day, soon after I get here, I go to grocery market.
I see worker taking milk and meat from refrigerator, and putting it in cart.
I ask retard what he is doing. He's telling me he's throwing it because it's expired.
Expired? Expired? It's perfectly fuckin fine food, right?
So I put it back in fridge.
Guy starts yip-yapping and pushes me, so I deliver him sexy kick into the vegetables. Little damage. Then I deliver a less sexy kick when he comes back at me.
5 guys jump me!
Mr. Big Manager is called. Big lush scene. Doesn't want to talk, just wants to call the cops.
Man, I didn't understand.
You call the cops because a guy doesn't want to throw perfectly fine fuckin food?
Back home, we discuss this thing!
I'm charged?
Interesting fuckin beginning.

Breakfast continues...

mrff
mgghr
Crazy shit!
Worse, I get here and the wife is all panicked and paranoid and pissed off.
She's mommy's princess, from a wealthy family and just jealous to death.
Thinks this is atrocious. Hates it!
So, it took me 4 years to sort of find what I thought was going to be a temporary solution.
I'm delivering newspapers and other bottom-of-barrel jobs.
And then I'm picking these scrapper bikes and fixing them.
And I found that extremely rewarding, to rescue shit and put it back to use.
And in the process I guess I evolved into fairly ardent and competent defendant of scrappers.

First place was on Dovercourt Street.* Like, I did not have a phone, no advertising.
Meanwhile, my woman worked for Air Canada so I flew for free everywhere on the planet.
A really groovy lifestyle.
So I would go travel for weeks or months and come back. And as soon as I opened the door, like people just smelled me and came banging. I couldn't believe it.

* In the late 80s, Toronto's west-end Dovercourt neighbourhood - a few minutes' bicycle ride from the current Bicycle Clinic - was a first-generation Portuguese immigrant community. Igor didn't quite fit in. If the steadily building mountain of bikes didn't keep the cops busy, the domestic battles between Igor and his wife certainly did. The charges accumulated.

So - typical - the ex kicked me out of the house in 91. She had crazy brain waves going off and she called the cops on me.
She was bright and cute and all but I don't really like girls that think they are above what I think they are.
I had to get rid of her.

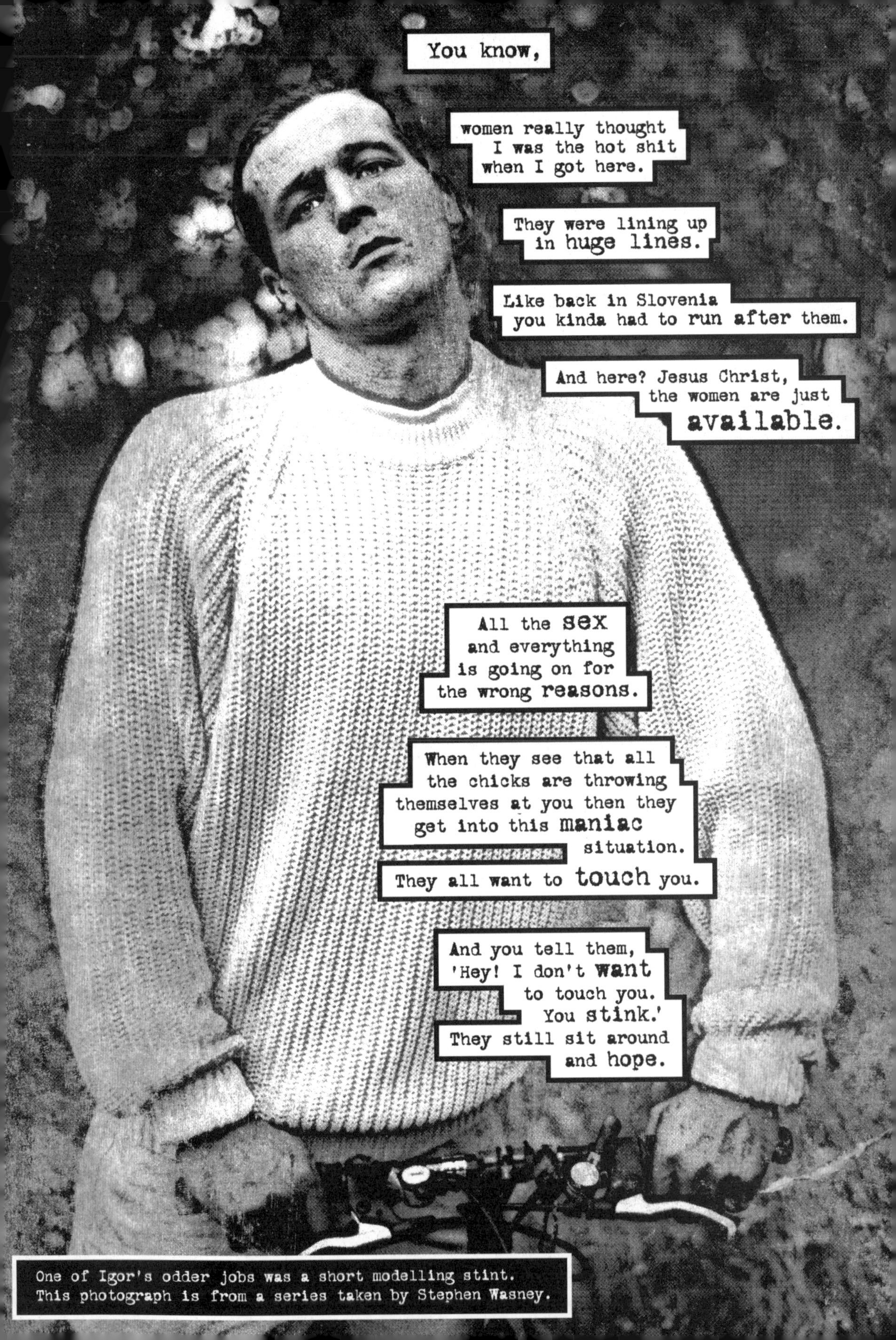
You know,
women really thought I was the hot shit when I got here.
They were lining up in huge lines.
Like back in Slovenia you kinda had to run after them.
And here? Jesus Christ, the women are just available.
All the sex and everything is going on for the wrong reasons.
When they see that all the chicks are throwing themselves at you then they get into this maniac situation.
They all want to touch you.
And you tell them, 'Hey! I don't want to touch you. You stink.'
They still sit around and hope.

One of Igor's odder jobs was a short modelling stint.
This photograph is from a series taken by Stephen Wasney.

The Bicycle Clinic I, 986 Queen Street West, 1992-1996
But even still, times were down, prosperity was down.
And then in 92 I opened the door on 986 Queen...
...and it was beyond. Absolutely beyond.

Igor inaugurated the place by getting nailed with his first drug charge in 92. He was busted with a quantity of marijuana. A year later, the cops swept in and charged him with posession of stolen property. More on that later.

THE BICYCLE CLINIC
BICYCLE REPAIRS
986

10, 15 years ago
in neighbourhood?

There was nothing,
just a **burnt-down** area.

Oh, it was horrendous, right?
It was just **third world country**.

There were people
with no money
for a **potato**.

People were
ignorant and
retarded.

NO EXIT
FUCK

Photo by Kevin Steele

West Queen Street West didn't notice the recession of the early 90s, mostly because it was always in a recession. Igor's store was near the cryptically named 999 Queen Street West, Toronto's longstanding mental institution, first opened in the 1850s when it was more descriptively called the Provincial Lunatic Asylum. In 1992, the area's mean household income was about 40% below the Canadian norm.

Now in my early stages when I was going to garage sales in Scarborough? * I would have trailers.
I would put bikes on me and on trailers and bring up to 8 bicycles back across city from east end.
Tourists were taking shots.
Basically people were laughing at me.

* Scarborough was at the time a vast, low-income east-end town adjacent to Toronto. They have since amalgamated.

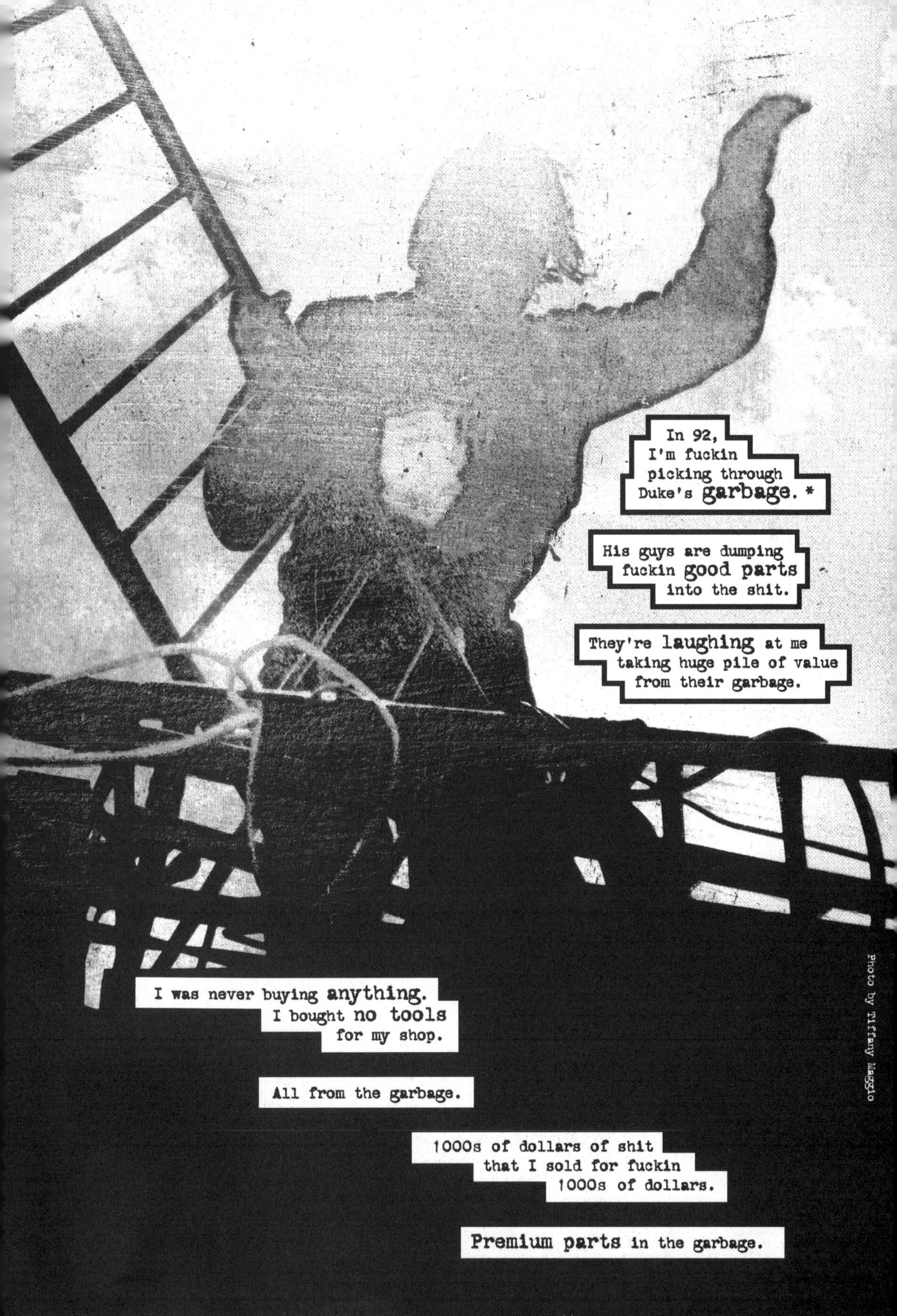
In 92,
I'm fuckin
picking through
Duke's garbage. *
His guys are dumping
fuckin good parts
into the shit.
They're laughing at me
taking huge pile of value
from their garbage.
I was never buying anything.
I bought no tools
for my shop.
All from the garbage.
1000s of dollars of shit
that I sold for fuckin
1000s of dollars.
Premium parts in the garbage.

Photo by Tiffany Maggio

* Duke's was at the time the cycling shop in Toronto.

The following images are taken from footage shot by filmmaker Anthony Jorindia - not the first person to point a camera at Igor, but certainly one of the most prolific. He taped over 20 hours of material during 1997.

Flashing back to the good old days...

Meanwhile,
I could not ever dream of the residue
of the attention.
People were waiting like Nazi death camp,
lining up for my services.
The cash.
It was great.
It required heavy
determination.
The customers, of course, most of them were
uneducated, not well behaved and not
equipped with a
brain function.
So you can imagine.

But I was feeling
really good.
Because I wasn't a
misfit.

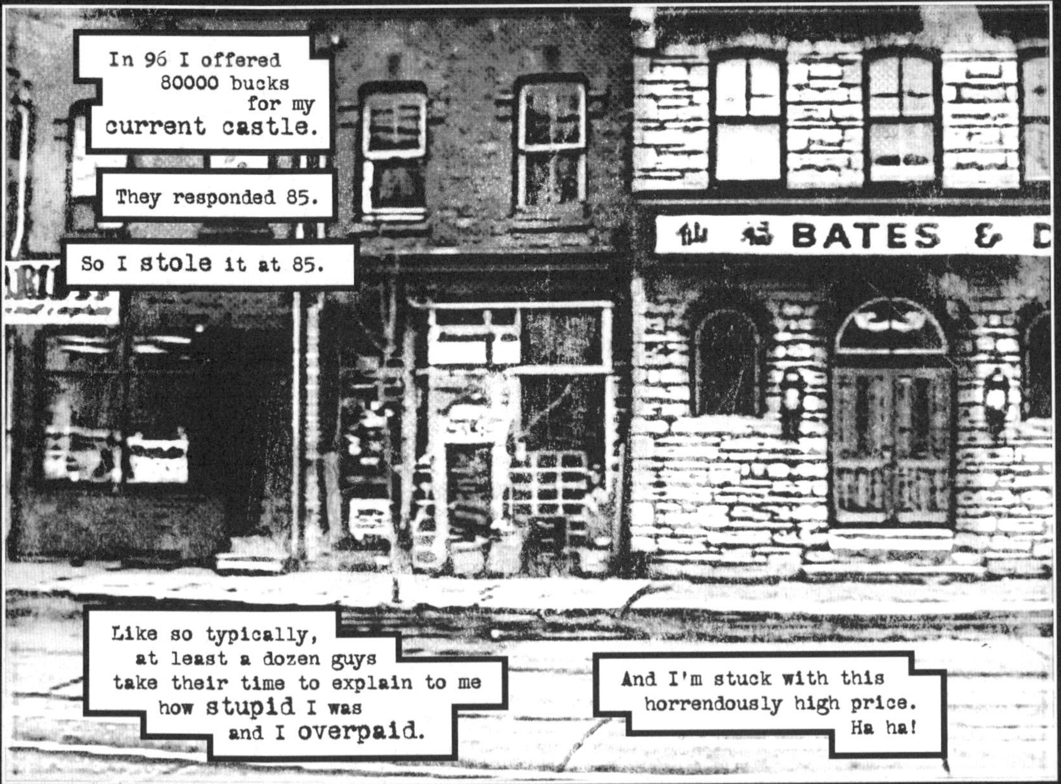
In 96 I offered 80000 bucks for my current castle.
They responded 85.
So I stole it at 85.
BATES & D
Like so typically, at least a dozen guys take their time to explain to me how stupid I was and I overpaid.
And I'm stuck with this horrendously high price. Ha ha!

Once a union burial hall for Polish and Slovakian immigrants, Bates & Dodds funeral home featured in the acrimonious divorce proceedings between one Dean Hallett and the scorned Mrs. Hallett. She was granted the property beside the funeral home, and listed it for $85,000. Igor's mother and aunt helped him with the down payment.

Oh, store was a business!
From business perspective it was insanely successful.
IGOR RACE READY BICYCLES AT
PUPPIES FOR SALE
WHITE
TAN
Insanely beautiful.

Despite the lingering issues with 986 Queen Street West, Igor was accorded a second-hand licence - #B72-2904658 ("records, bicycles and household goods") - and the Bicycle Clinic II at 927 Queen Street West was born.

OPEN
Shop is never closed or open.
If someone manages to get me down to the door...
STAFF
Moments later, back downstairs...
These parts are broken. I give you 5 bucks.
We're in Canada. Where you from? Bolivia?
ha ha ha
phillipines.
Holy fuck! Close enough. How much you want for them?
6 bucks.
Ah! We gentleman or what? Tough fuckin negotiator.

Later still...

That fuckin war shit? I don't wanna go home man. They're all villagers. They're banging away all over the place. Little places I never heard of - banging away!
Serbs, they...
...did you see where I put the axle?
Unbelievable...
Us eastern Europeans - we're proofed against any shit you throw at us.
STAFF
We're way tougher. Way tougher.
I'm building my logic according to the society I'm coming from, right?

Customer relation procedures were set from day one...

Get out of here with that bike, man. It doesn't make me happy.
!
You don't want to pay for well-established shit?
Marrrghhhh!
STAF
And...
I'm not your father or your lover to be responsible for what your fuckin business looks like.
Meantime, as your old-time bicycle guy, you've been pulling my balls for 2 years now.
You're gonna be rotten before I get any money out of you, buddy! And this is not fair!
More still...
This is how the industry works: you're supposed to keep paying money. Money money money money.
Money money money money money money money.
Always, all the time, keep rolling.
Every time you see your bike man, you're supposed to say, 'Please, take some more!'
No bulging eyes, no crying.

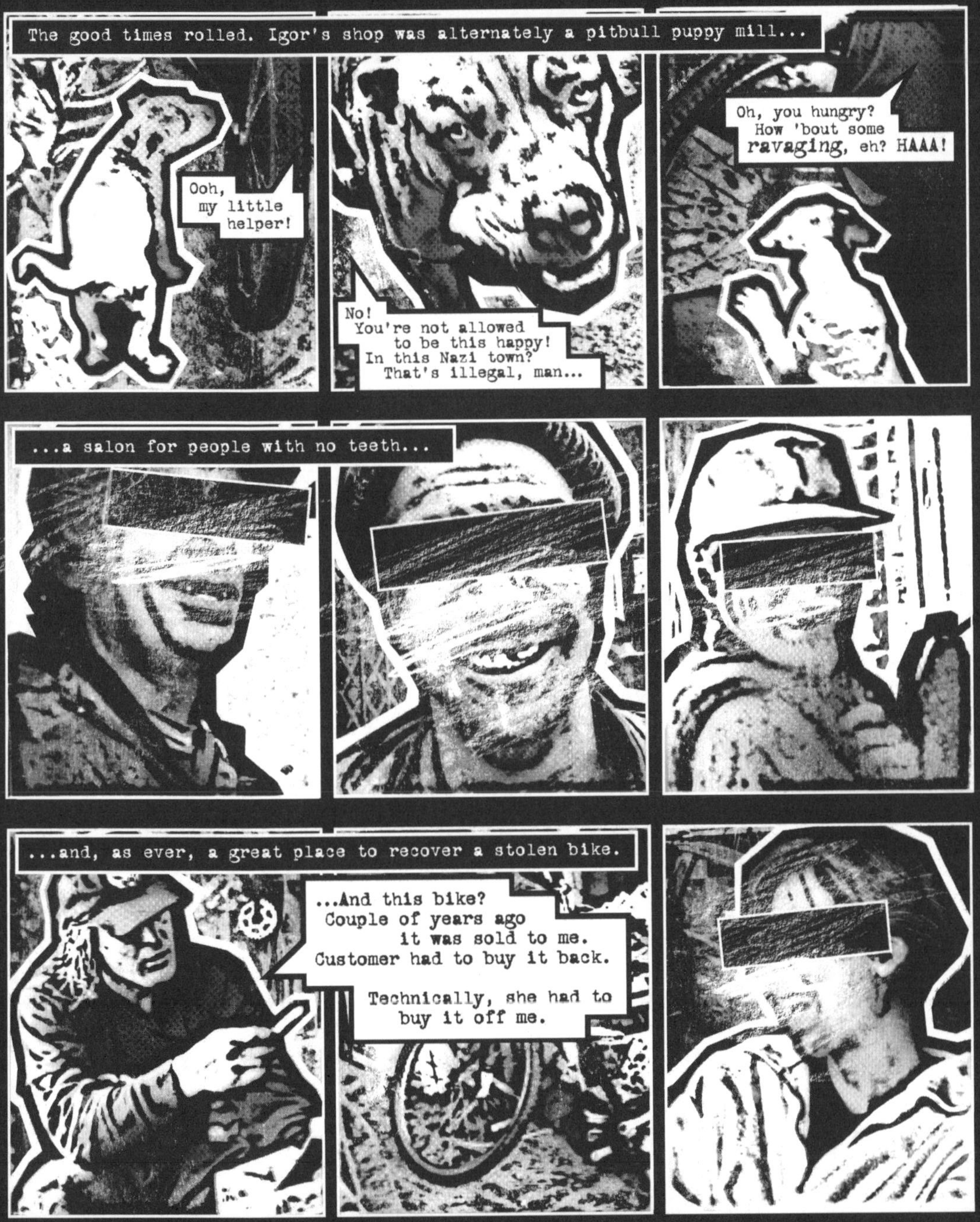
The good times rolled. Igor's shop was alternately a pitbull puppy mill...
Ooh, my little helper!
No! You're not allowed to be this happy! In this Nazi town? That's illegal, man...
Oh, you hungry? How 'bout some ravaging, eh? HAAA!
...a salon for people with no teeth...
...and, as ever, a great place to recover a stolen bike.
...And this bike? Couple of years ago it was sold to me. Customer had to buy it back.
Technically, she had to buy it off me.

If the store fitted seamlessly into the 'hood when Igor moved in, by 2002 that deal was all but over...

OPEN
CLAFOUTI
The mess accumulated...
...local artsy residents grew up and opened shops and cafés.

Consistent lobbying led to a change in zoning laws, which was shortly followed by 999 Queen Street West's long-promised makeover: it is now a sprawling neighbour-friendly facility called CAMH - the Centre for Addiction and Mental Health.

Transforming Lives Here
camh
www.camh.net
416 535-8501
All this begat, among other things, high-end fish and chips...
CHIPPY'S
Fish & Chips
...and, most significantly...

...the Drake.
THE DRAKE HOTEL
A flophouse turned boutique hotel cum nightclub, if any one thing remade the Queen Street West strip, it was this place.
COFFEE
DRAKE YOU HO THIS IS ALL YOUR

Once upon a time, Igor owned this strip...

I'm glad that people here are so poor.
Because if people start making 5 times as much money here...
I'm fuckin screwed. I'm out. I'm finito.

Flash forward to The Lakeview Lunch...

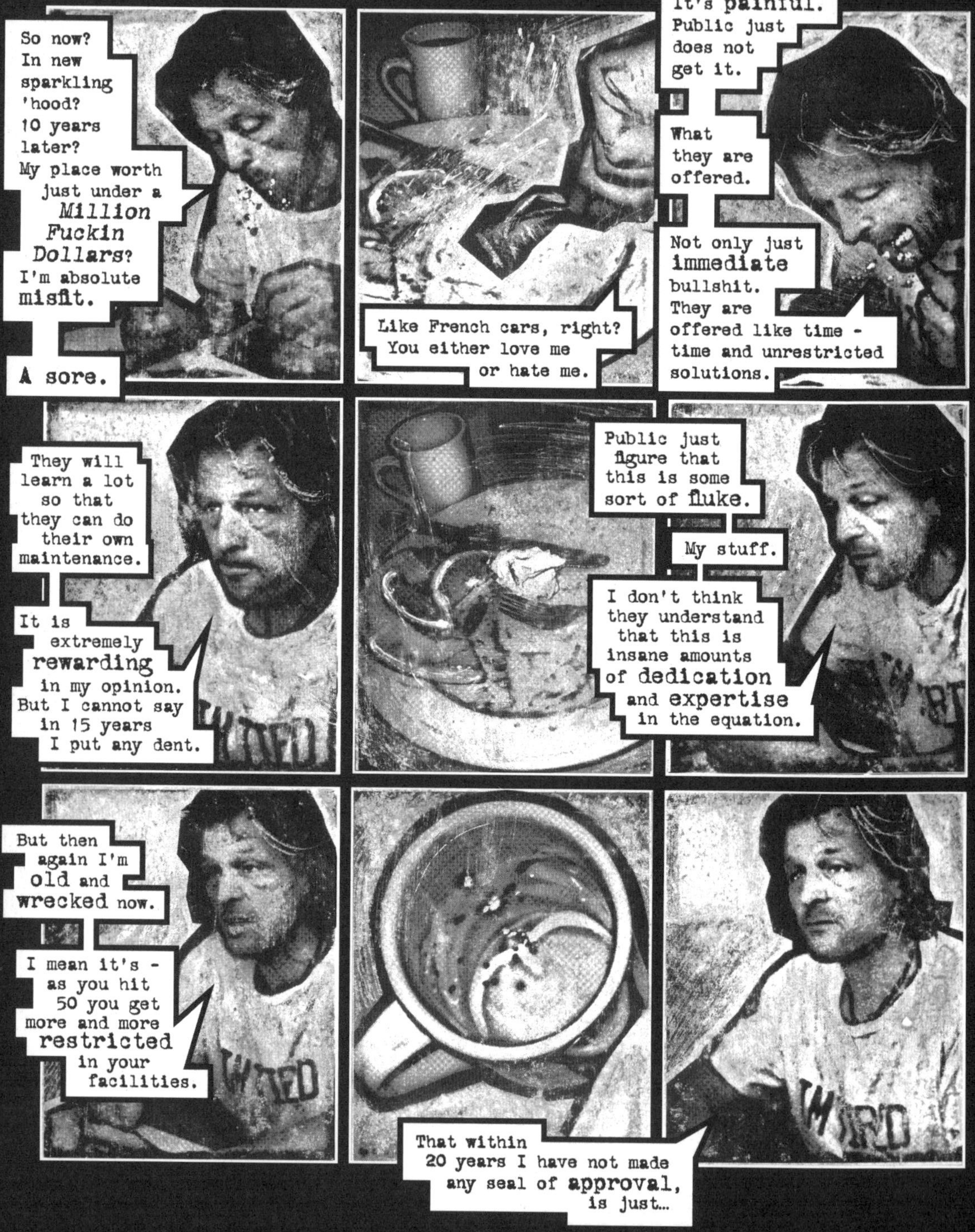

So now? In new sparkling 'hood? 10 years later? My place worth just under a Million Fuckin Dollars? I'm absolute misfit.
A sore.
Like French cars, right? You either love me or hate me.
It's painful. Public just does not get it.
What they are offered.
Not only just immediate bullshit. They are offered like time - time and unrestricted solutions.
They will learn a lot so that they can do their own maintenance.
It is extremely rewarding in my opinion. But I cannot say in 15 years I put any dent.
Public just figure that this is some sort of fluke.
My stuff.
I don't think they understand that this is insane amounts of dedication and expertise in the equation.
But then again I'm old and wrecked now.
I mean it's - as you hit 50 you get more and more restricted in your facilities.
That within 20 years I have not made any seal of approval, is just...

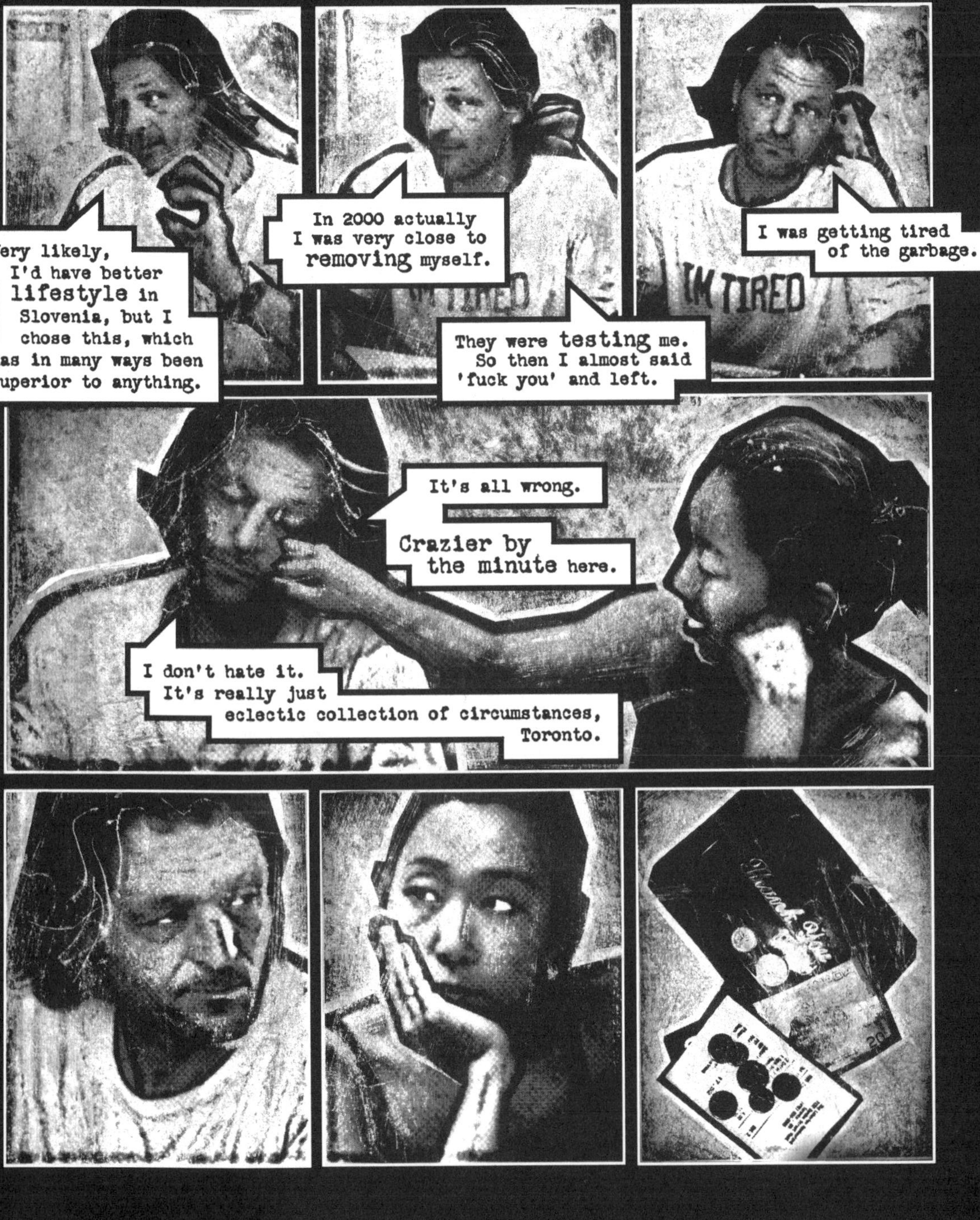
Very likely, I'd have better lifestyle in Slovenia, but I chose this, which has in many ways been superior to anything.
In 2000 actually I was very close to removing myself.
IM TIRED
They were testing me. So then I almost said 'fuck you' and left.
I was getting tired of the garbage.
IM TIRED
It's all wrong.
Crazier by the minute here.
I don't hate it. It's really just eclectic collection of circumstances, Toronto.

Photo by Stephen Wasney, 1991

Court Interlude

Old City Hall courthouse
June 2007 - 13 months before major bust

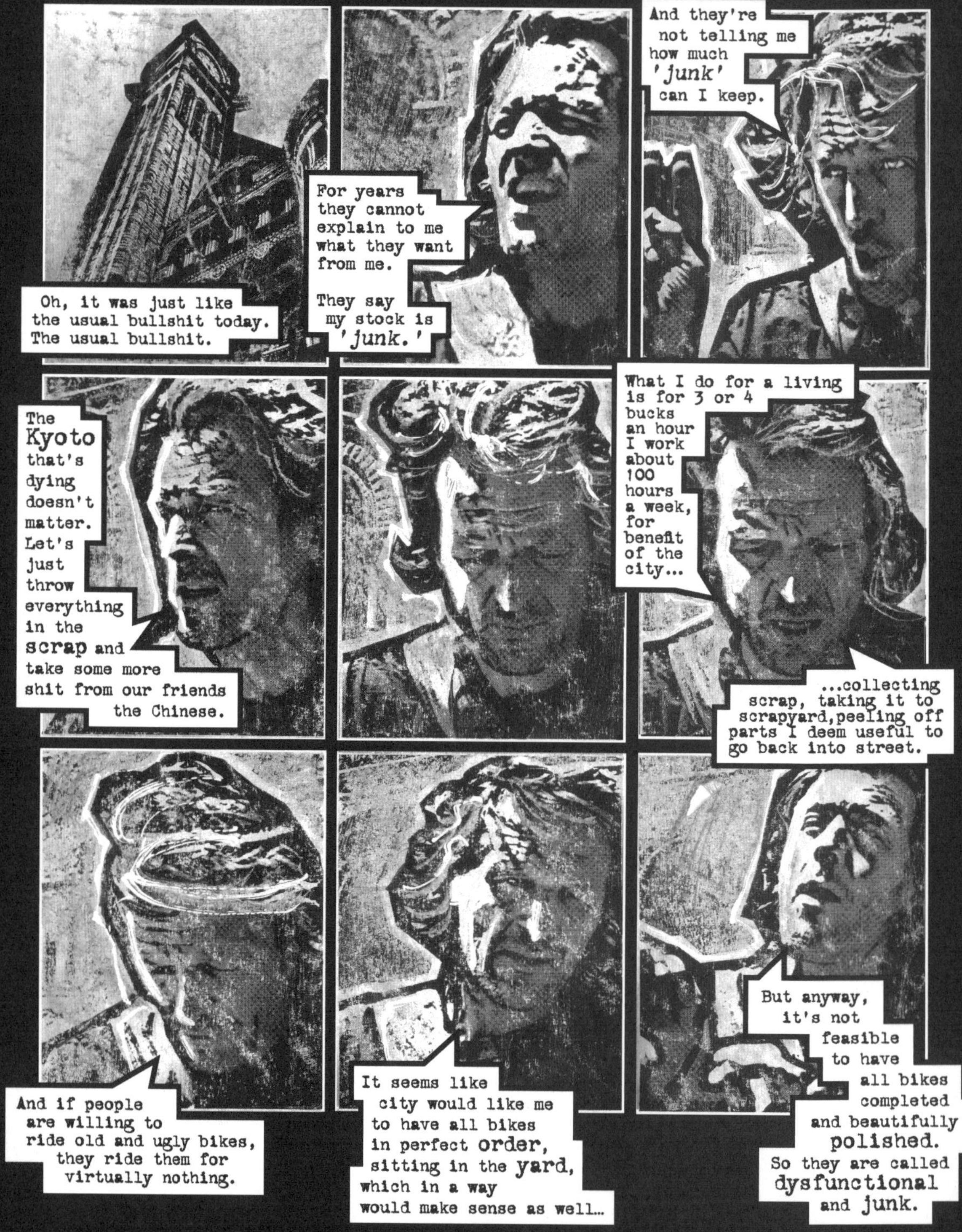
Oh, it was just like the usual bullshit today. The usual bullshit.
For years they cannot explain to me what they want from me.
They say my stock is 'junk.'
And they're not telling me how much 'junk' can I keep.
The Kyoto that's dying doesn't matter. Let's just throw everything in the scrap and take some more shit from our friends the Chinese.
What I do for a living is for 3 or 4 bucks an hour I work about 100 hours a week, for benefit of the city...
...collecting scrap, taking it to scrapyard, peeling off parts I deem useful to go back into street.
And if people are willing to ride old and ugly bikes, they ride them for virtually nothing.
It seems like city would like me to have all bikes in perfect order, sitting in the yard, which in a way would make sense as well...
But anyway, it's not feasible to have all bikes completed and beautifully polished.
So they are called dysfunctional and junk.

Yeah, Harry the lawyer says they just want yard to be neat.
Even though in between the trees above and 3 walls of neighbours, you can't see, even if you're from CIA.
I don't know who is getting hurt from 'unorderly garden' of mine.
I guess dealing with scrap is just not desired. This society - gas masks are imminent.
And we're in hurry to wear them.
I tell them, 'It's not junk. It's my stuff.'
Just bikes that need modest amounts of work.
I have to throw them all away.

PART II

Photo by Tiffany Maggio

July 2007 - 1 year before major bust
chug
chug
EAGER

♪
"...filosofa,
ragioni...
e ver! vo via!..."
♪

CHAPTER 4: CALL ME A PEDOPHILE OR WHATEVER. JUST GIVE ME MY STUFF BACK AND FUCK OFF

Oh,
fuckin **right**, man!

YARD SALE
Gilmour Avenue,
Toronto's west end
clink
How much is this scissors?
dunno.
They didn't instruct you as to the preciousness...?
no.

Precious things...
So how you gonna do garage sale if you don't...
um, maybe a buck?
oh, there he is.
yup?
Your lady estimated buck each.
nah - 2 bucks for the barber scissors.
that little one's probably worth 25 bucks...
I take it to my drawer and keep it there, and it will be good.
And those bikes are not for sale, right...?
i gave a guy that bike. i don't think he wants to sell it.

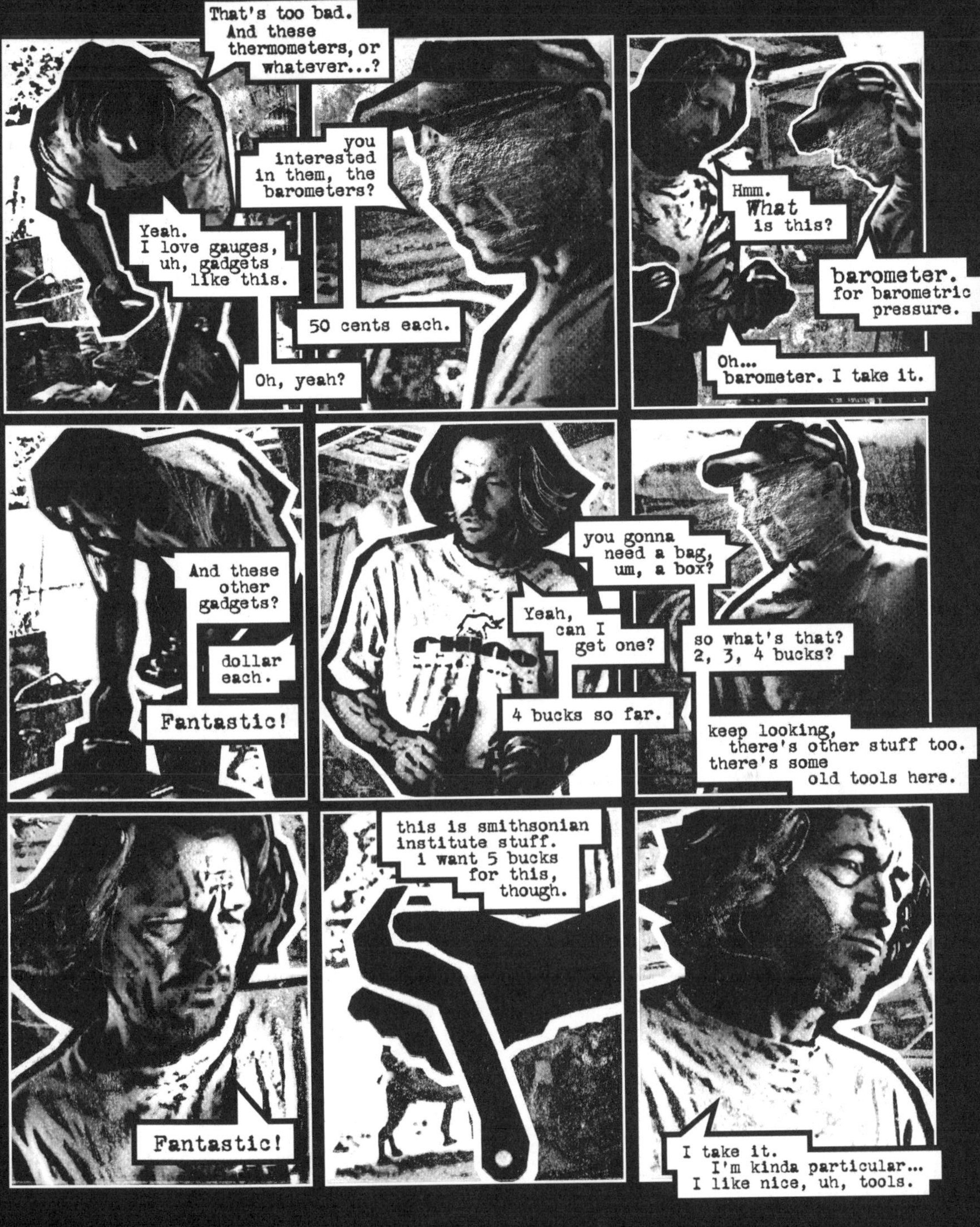
That's too bad. And these thermometers, or whatever...?
you interested in them, the barometers?
Yeah. I love gauges, uh, gadgets like this.
50 cents each.
Oh, yeah?
Hmm. What is this?
barometer. for barometric pressure.
Oh... barometer. I take it.
And these other gadgets?
dollar each.
Fantastic!
you gonna need a bag, um, a box?
Yeah, can I get one?
4 bucks so far.
so what's that? 2, 3, 4 bucks?
keep looking, there's other stuff too. there's some old tools here.
Fantastic!
this is smithsonian institute stuff. i want 5 bucks for this, though.
I take it. I'm kinda particular... I like nice, uh, tools.

well, bud, you're getting yourself some good stuff.
Sure, sure.
And this?
dollar.
...$13 so far.
So, I've seen it all, you think, or...?
there's old hinges and stuff like that here.
Fantastic. I'll take them.
Minutes later...
$
$
Whoa!
That scooter there is more than couple of bucks?
okay, sure. 2 bucks.

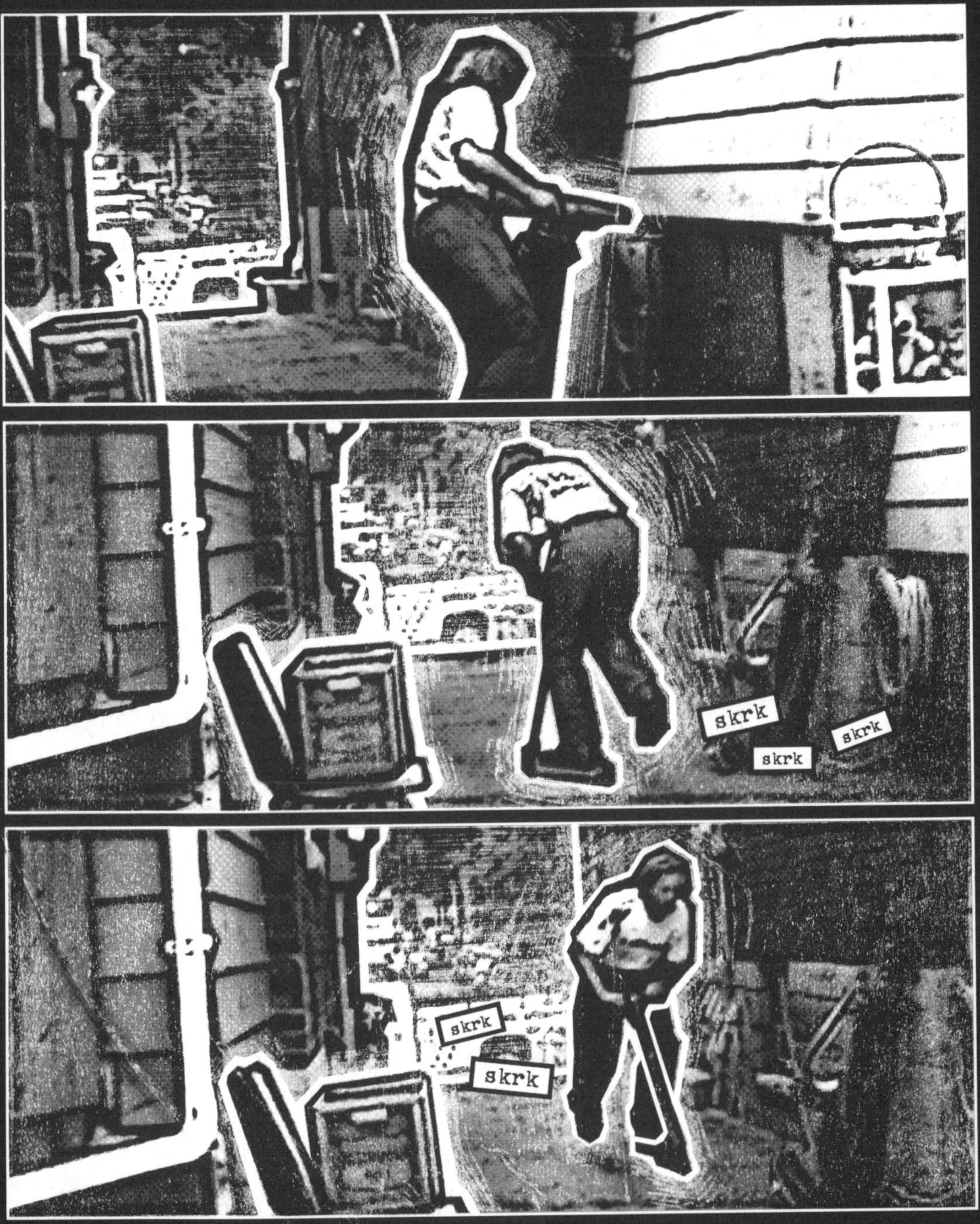
skrk
skrk
skrk
skrk
skrk

!!!
!!!
oh my. never seen that before...
why do i think you're going to make a sculpture out of this stuff?
Yeah - that's *exactly* what I'm going to do, brother.
because i'm an artist too.
if not, at least you could recover your money from it one way or another.
you wanna see a beautiful tool, bro?
Huh?
What it's...???
2 bucks.
Okay. I take it.

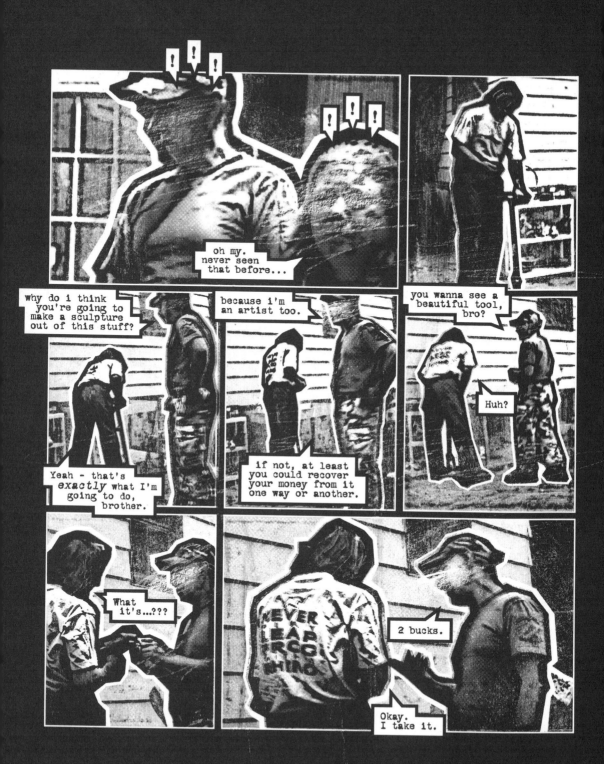

$27 later...
skrk
skrk
skrk
skrk

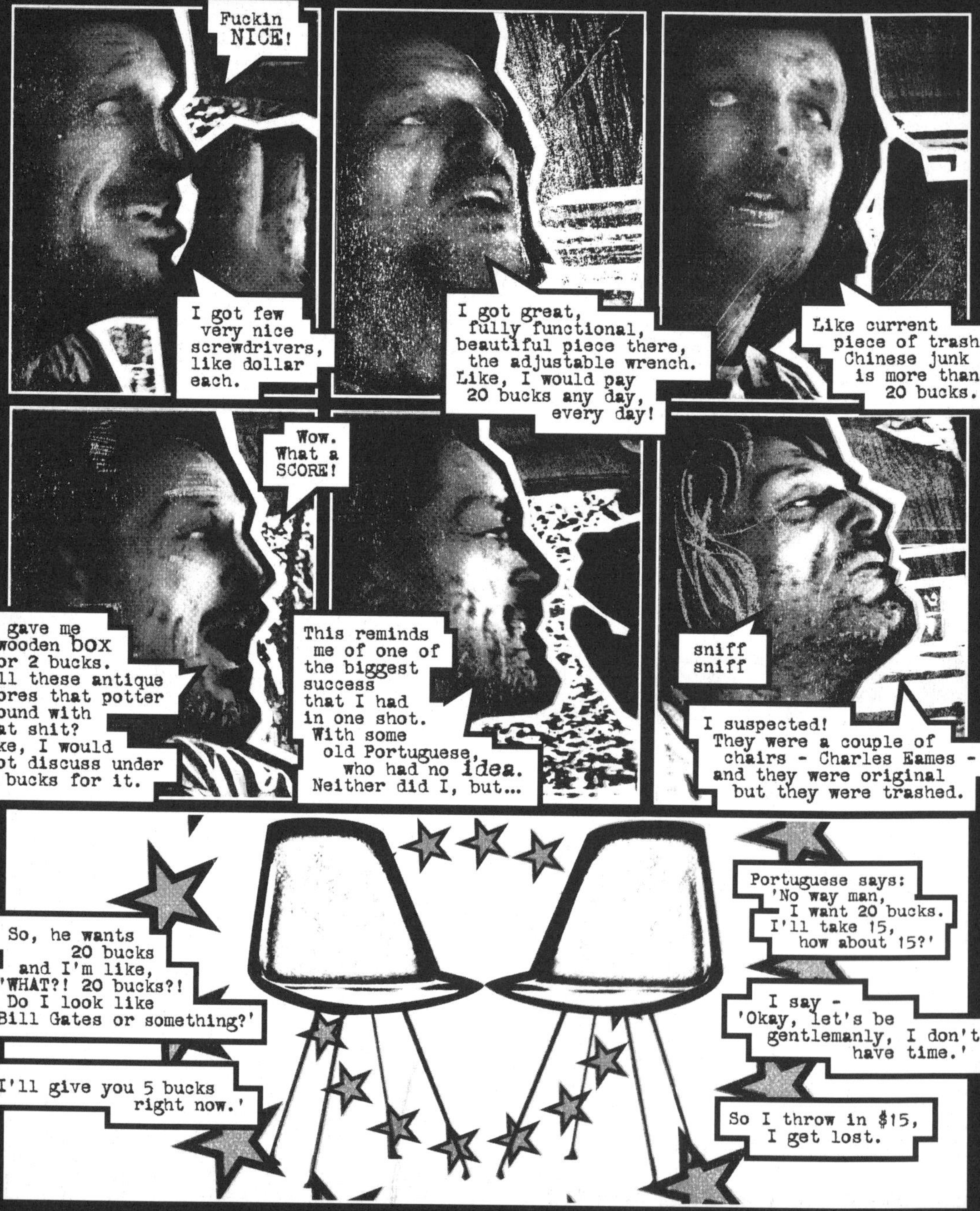

Fuckin NICE!
I got few very nice screwdrivers, like dollar each.
I got great, fully functional, beautiful piece there, the adjustable wrench. Like, I would pay 20 bucks any day, every day!
Like current piece of trash Chinese junk is more than 20 bucks.
Wow. What a SCORE!
He gave me a wooden box for 2 bucks. All these antique stores that potter around with that shit? Like, I would not discuss under 20 bucks for it.
This reminds me of one of the biggest success that I had in one shot. With some old Portuguese, who had no idea. Neither did I, but...
sniff sniff
I suspected! They were a couple of chairs - Charles Eames - and they were original but they were trashed.
So, he wants 20 bucks and I'm like, 'WHAT?! 20 bucks?! Do I look like Bill Gates or something?'
'I'll give you 5 bucks right now.'
Portuguese says: 'No way man, I want 20 bucks. I'll take 15, how about 15?'
I say - 'Okay, let's be gentlemanly, I don't have time.'
So I throw in $15, I get lost.

I stop in front of shop and drop chairs. TTC is passing by and people are POURING off TTC and everybody wants them.
*
Wait... is that pig there?
...
No.
Okay, so everybody wants chairs but nobody wants to pay.
Everybody's offering me 40 to 80, and I thought okay, 40 to 80 multiplied means good.
So then some Japanese dude comes and throws a big tantrum because I said no.
He goes, 'I'll give you 200 bucks right now.'
I say, 'NO! I have not owned them for long enough to enjoy myself.'
The truth is I was going to give them away fast because my Dogs - meaning my helpers - would fuckin trash them...
Oh, shit. Look!

* The Toronto Transit Commission, or TTC, is the city's public transportation system.

Minutes later...

Fuckin SCORE!
A hat! Totally dysfunctional, like only buck and a half. And this beautiful hand-stitched shit, for buck and a half.
Killer! Oooo! Faaan-tastic!
That's pretty good. 2 fruitful yard sales. I love yard sale.
"...toronto real-estate prices are skyrocketing, although the subprime mortgage crisis in the united states threatens..."
Mm-hmm. Sure, sure.
Fantastic. Cruising around, snatching sh-tuff...
Ohhhh! Here we go...

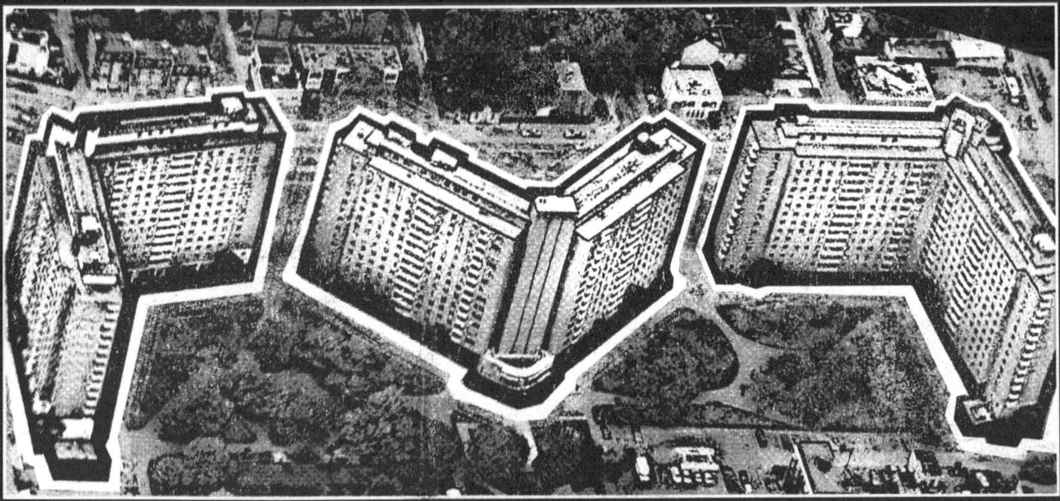

MOSS PARK APARTMENTS

This is the Moss Park housing project, in Toronto's east end. The informal summer market is renowned for offering some of the city's more brazen bargains.

How much are these?
those? 10 bucks a pair.
I got a kid that's 12 years old. I wonder if that's his size now... *
those are size 6, these are size 7.

* The kid Igor is referring to is his son, born in 1995 to a Canadian woman.

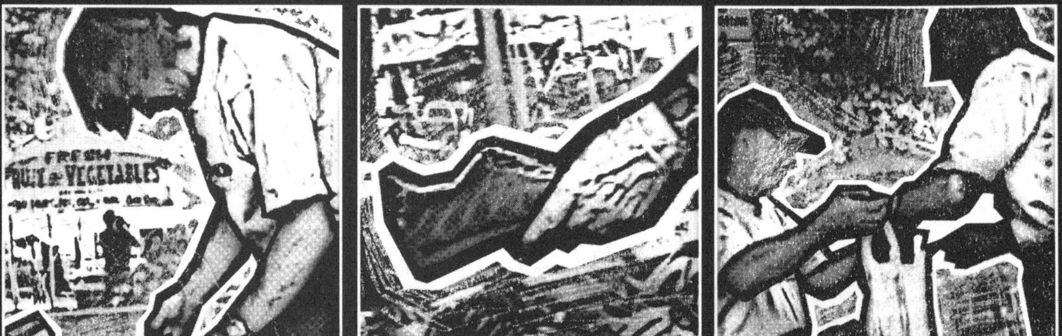
Cops. Pigs. Everywhere.
Fuckin everywhere.
POLICE

The cops. For years they have been sitting outside the store. They have been sitting and watching.
I have been very puzzled why, and how come they haven't taken me down.
That's the biggest puzzle.
It's a combination probably of them being slop bags. And the store. It's a pond. And they are predator.
It's more than an adequate exchange for them to let me do my shit, and they can keep snapping as much as they want.
And I tell you, they're not snapping all that hard.
It's like, 'Igor, he may be a piece of junk, but he's useful to us.'
PAWN-STO
BUY-SELL-TRADE!
CAMERAS
Now this is all hot, right? All hot. Hundreds and hundreds of bikes, all hot.
But nobody else but Igor is being mentioned in this city.

1993 - The First Great Bust

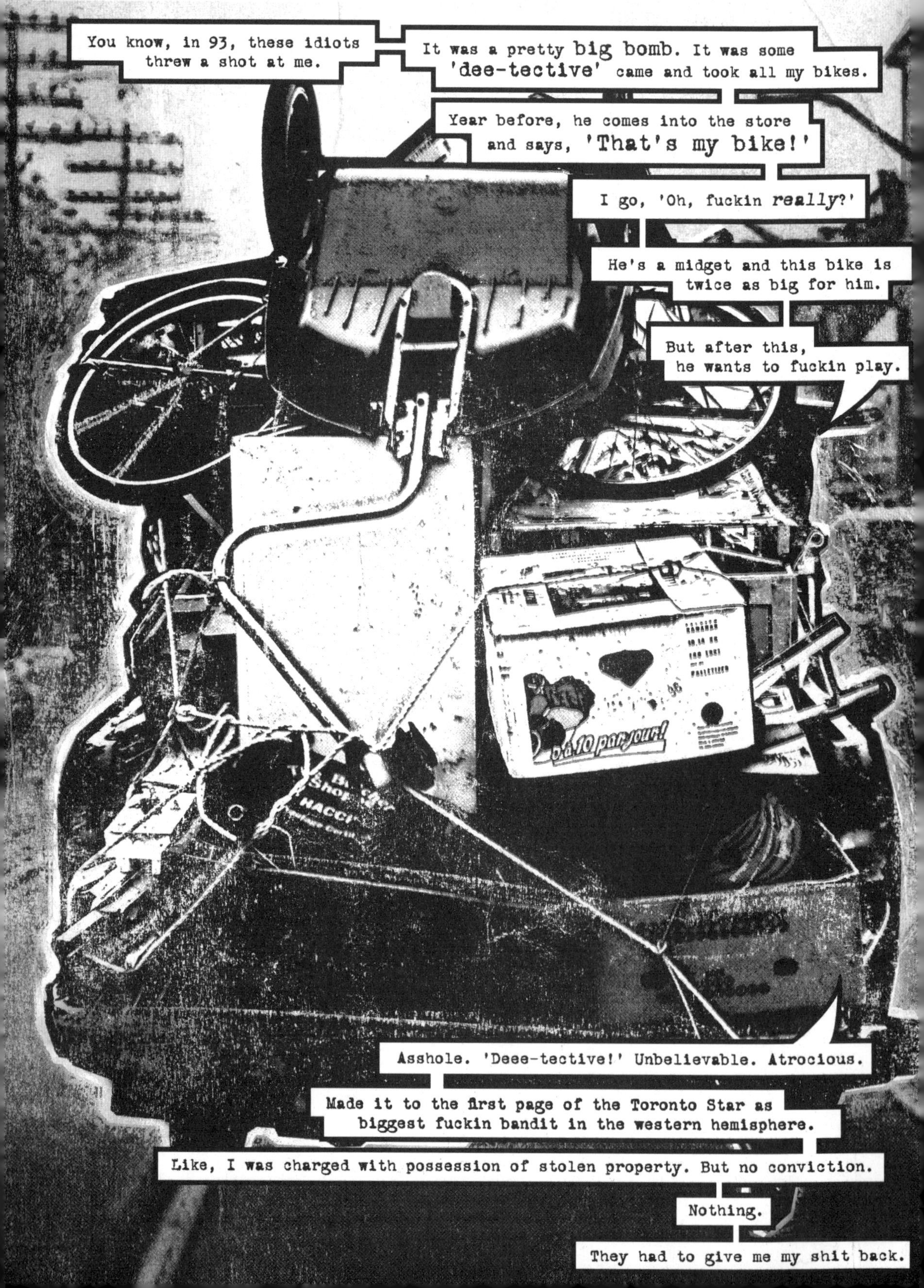

You know, in 93, these idiots threw a shot at me.
It was a pretty big bomb. It was some 'dee-tective' came and took all my bikes.
Year before, he comes into the store and says, 'That's my bike!'
I go, 'Oh, fuckin *really*?'
He's a midget and this bike is twice as big for him.
But after this, he wants to fuckin play.
Asshole. 'Deee-tective!' Unbelievable. Atrocious.
Made it to the first page of the Toronto Star as biggest fuckin bandit in the western hemisphere.
Like, I was charged with possession of stolen property. But no conviction.
Nothing.
They had to give me my shit back.

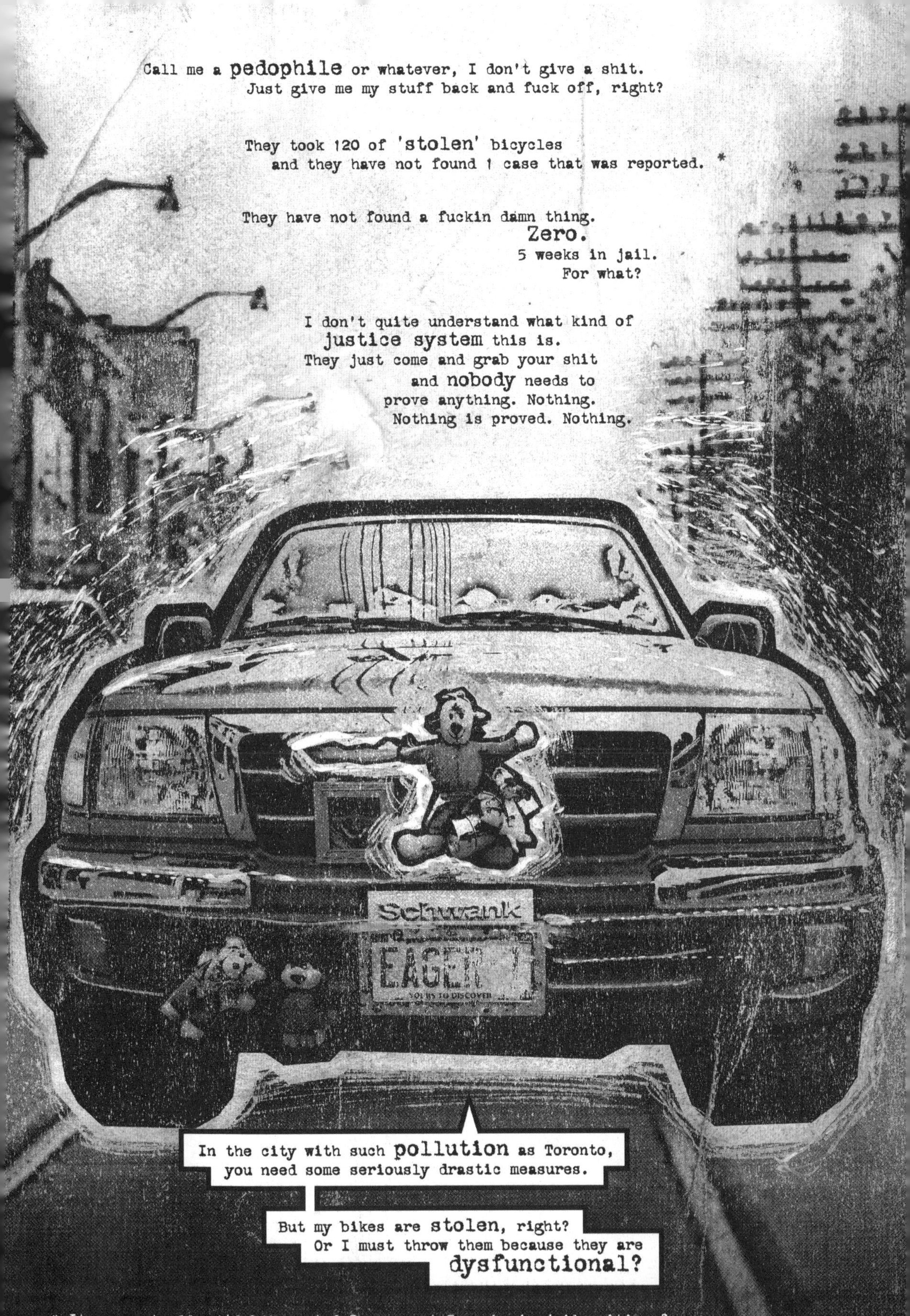
Call me a pedophile or whatever, I don't give a shit.
Just give me my stuff back and fuck off, right?
They took 120 of 'stolen' bicycles
and they have not found 1 case that was reported. *
They have not found a fuckin damn thing.
Zero.
5 weeks in jail.
For what?
I don't quite understand what kind of
justice system this is.
They just come and grab your shit
and nobody needs to
prove anything. Nothing.
Nothing is proved. Nothing.
Schwank
YOURS TO DISCOVER
In the city with such pollution as Toronto,
you need some seriously drastic measures.
But my bikes are stolen, right?
Or I must throw them because they are
dysfunctional?

* It was actually 140 bikes. And Igor spent 5 weeks in jail waiting for the police to complete their paperwork. Not one of the charges stuck.

Around the corner...

Whoa! Babushkas!
! ! !
! ! !
Did you want some help with that scrap there?
this garbage?
Yeah, that's the question.
Better this way, girls. It's cheaper for taxpayer.
?
clunk

Still on the prowl...

2 bucks of scrap. But that's 2 minutes of labour, right?
♪
"l'insana parola, o numi, sperdete! al seno d'un padre, la figlia rendete..."
♪
Lookee here. Dumpster time.
Do we want this? Maybe.

Perfectly good
old shoe.
Full box of
envelopes.
Wasteful
shit...
Perfectly fine box
of plastic cups.
Fuckin waste, huh?
Maybe I leave
it on street
for people...
Waste.
Typical Canadian.
Brain-dead
toothless loser.

This kind of loser, his garbage is pouring from the container and beyond.
Yup. Poor thing.
Vulgar display of purchasing power.
Like for impoverished loser like me this of course is fantastic. I don't need to waste...
I don't need to have. Like I'm not interested in having things, right?
Like chicks right? You really don't want to fuck them all but...
...you want to be under the impression that you can grab them if you want to...
The option. It's all about the option...

Fuckin North America.

Shit pouring from the garbage
to point we never need to
make another thing. Ever!

People hand me their shit -
they *hand* it to me.
They leave it on street!

SALE FREE
SALE FREE
SALE FREE
SALE FREE
SALE FREE
MAXIMUM 40
But Igor's shit is all hot, right?
All hot.

All hot.

Photo by Tiffany Maggio

Cop Interlude
POLICE

Welcome to 14 Division, the single busiest police division in Canada, encompassing a dense sweep of the west end of Toronto including Igor's Bicycle Clinic.

here's the thing most people don't understand:
this neighbour-hood includes everyone from the portuguese fisherman who came here in the 1930s...
...to the art-school kid...
...to the long-term drug addict.
Robert Tajti, 14 Division Planner
we're busy - and that's not an excuse...
...but property theft is tough to prosecute.

if someone were to steal 10,000 bicycles? in canada, we can only prosecute those as individual cases of 'theft under 5,000 dollars.'
essentially, those bikes are the equivalent of 10,000 stolen mars bars.
nonetheless, we hear the complaints: 'you know that mr. kenk deals in hot bikes - you *send* us there! - so why don't you arrest him?'
TORONTO POLICE
well, we *don't* know that he's dealing in stolen property.
insofar as he complies with the terms of his second-hand licence - terms that are set by city legislators - we don't have a leg to stand on.
happily, in this country, there needs to be significant due process before we can charge someone with a crime.
for one thing, we need search warrants. and no judge will grant one based on rumour.
my counter-argument would be, if you assume he is dealing in stolen property, why are you at his place of business?

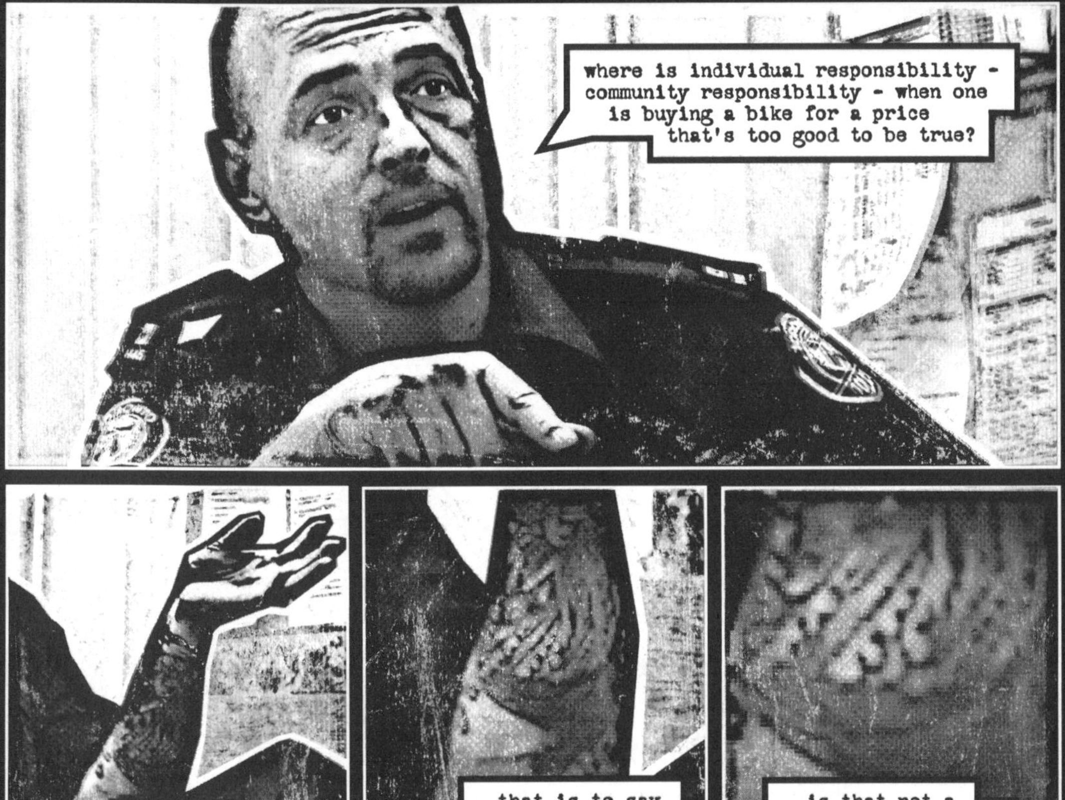
where is individual responsibility - community responsibility - when one is buying a bike for a price that's too good to be true?
based on prevailing assumptions...
...that is to say, the assumptions of many in the community...
...is that not a de facto case of stealing from your neighbour?
POLICE

CHAPTER 5: EVERYTHING'S STOLEN? WHY DON'T WE TALK SLIGHTLY LESS IMPRECISELY?

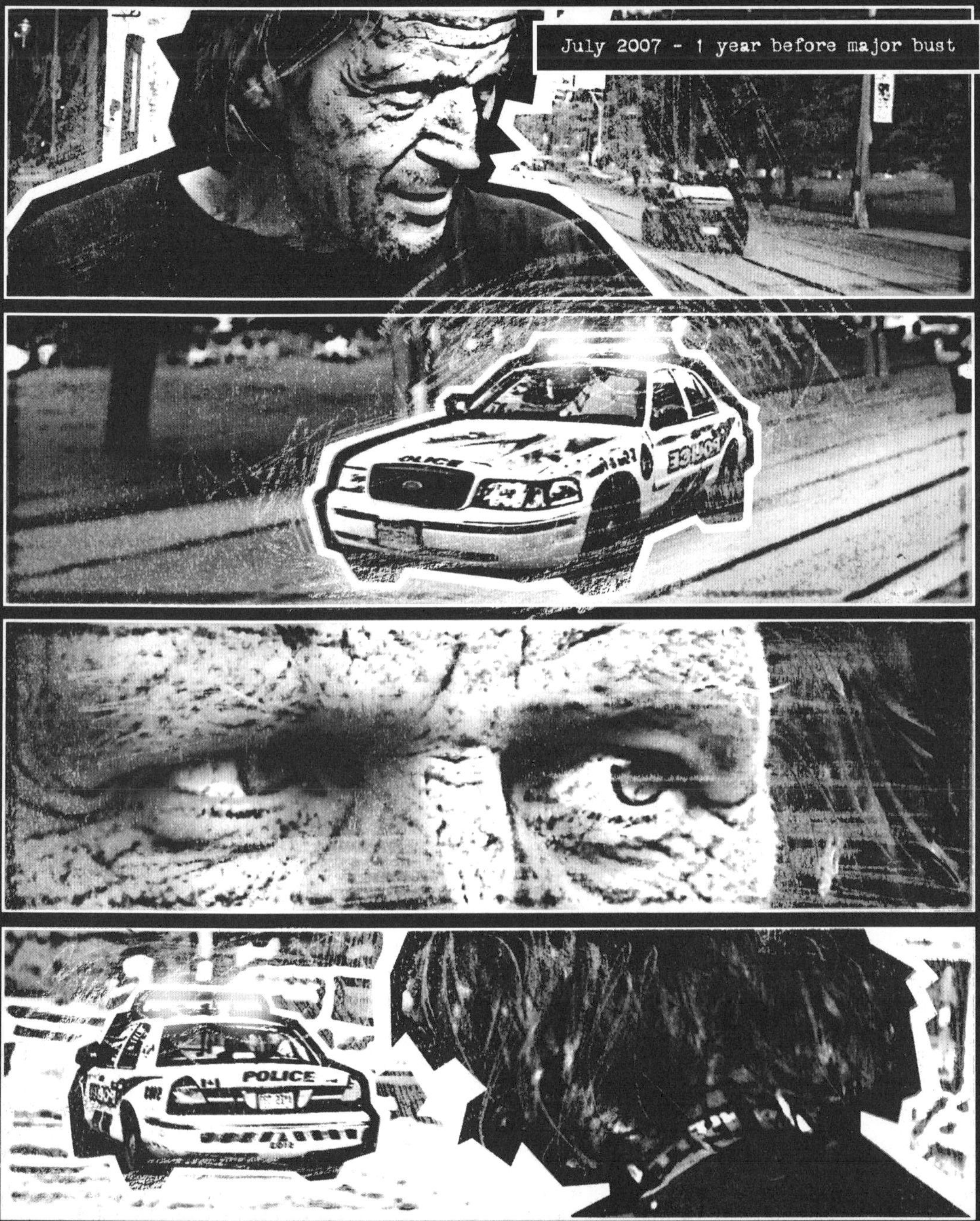
July 2007 - 1 year before major bust
POLICE

TRINITY BELLWOODS

Age
Height
Hair
Work Order Number
Type of Identification Shown
Vehicle Licence Number
75108

This is Igor's so-called Bible.

After the first big bust in 93, Igor claims to have become meticulous about recording his transactions, complying with the letter of the law, if not with its spirit.

According to the terms of Igor's second-hand licence, as long as the name, address and contact information of the vendor are entered into the Bible, the licence holder is not liable. The property must stand in the store for a 3-week waiting period. If it isn't claimed, Igor is free to sell.

It is a system not without its loopholes.

A thief?
Everything's stolen?
clap
clap
Why don't we talk slightly less imprecisely.

BICYCLE
CLINIC
CO-OP
Menu
get your fix...
flat tire members $10
non-members $15
tune-up $40
$10-$20
gear adjustments $10
wheel straightening $10-$30
chain
bottom bracket
detailing

From a certain eye, things may appear downside up.
But Public doesn't understand.
And cops don't begin to fuckin pretend to understand.
So...

Allow me to explain...
Public is miserable. You can see they are miserable.
You are talking to them and they're all whiny and they come and say, 'Oh I want to look at bikes.'
And it's like, dude, this is not a fuckin promenade.
When you have some form of idea of which direction you wanna work in, then come by and tell me, and we'll send you to that direction.
Hopefully by then I will start understanding who are you. Like is your brain non-existent? Is your head good just for the hairstyle?
I will think for you. Everything is going to be done for you. Allow me to be your butler. I will whore myself to death with pleasure.
So what it ends up as, basically, I'm a nickel-and-dime equivalent probably of those guys that go around and they fix companies.
Companies that have expenditures and have good revenues but need to be helped to steal even more money? And then the company survives?
I'm that guy.

So,
what I do is
basically
Dutch.
For 20-30 bucks,
I let the person
ride the whole
season.
They come when the
sun comes out, drop me
whatever, 100 bucks,
I give them the fuckin bike.
They come back and
get 60-70 bucks back
in the fall.
I mean lock
and bike and
whole works.
You can't
beat that.
I don't sell *anything*.
I don't peddle *anything*.
sqwrk
I tell Public
they should invest.
With prospect of using
bike for many years for
very little, and not
destroying it.
If they follow my path,
they won't suffer.

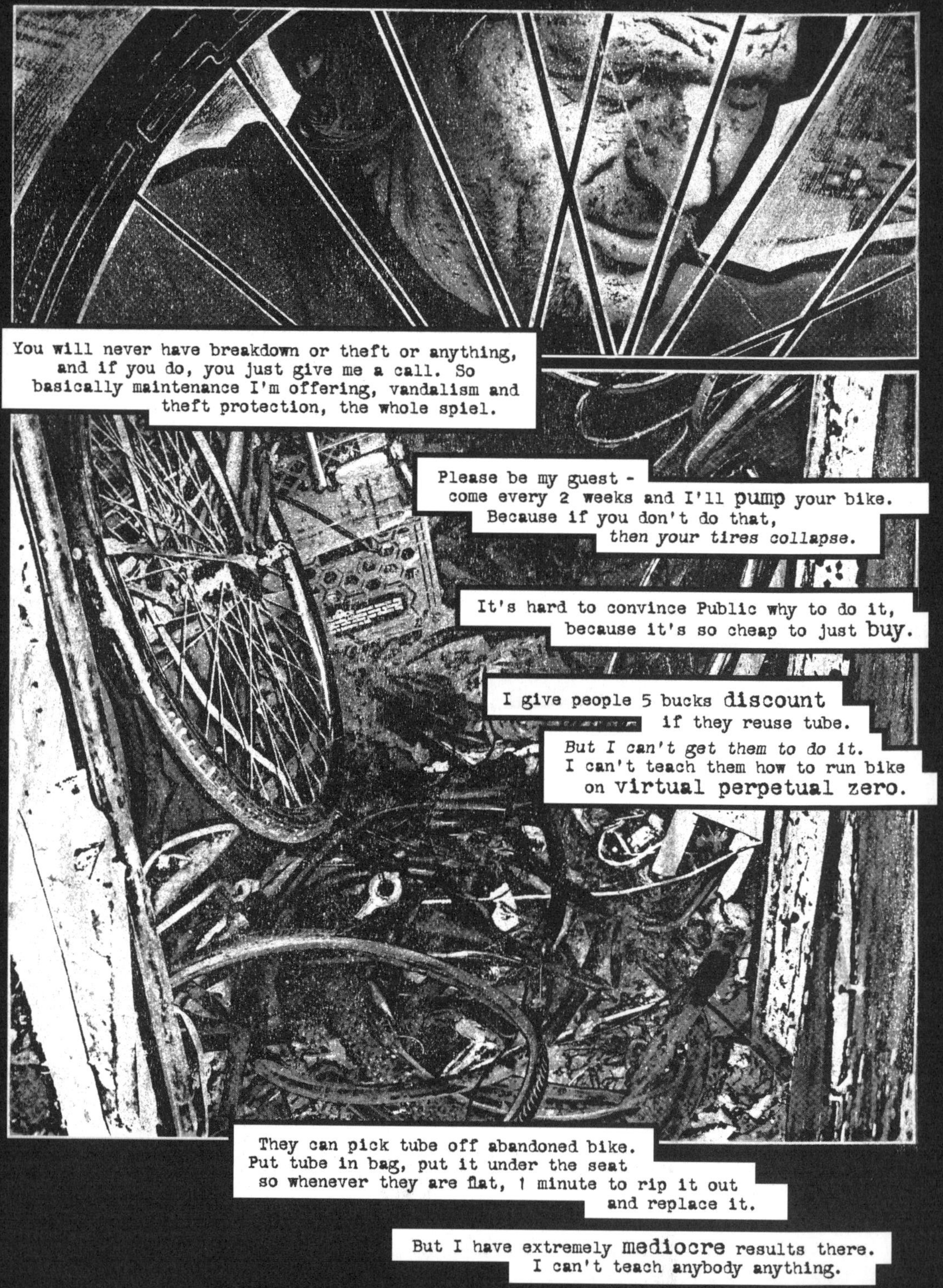
You will never have breakdown or theft or anything, and if you do, you just give me a call. So basically maintenance I'm offering, vandalism and theft protection, the whole spiel.
Please be my guest - come every 2 weeks and I'll pump your bike. Because if you don't do that, then your tires collapse.
It's hard to convince Public why to do it, because it's so cheap to just buy.
I give people 5 bucks discount if they reuse tube.
But I can't get them to do it. I can't teach them how to run bike on virtual perpetual zero.
They can pick tube off abandoned bike. Put tube in bag, put it under the seat so whenever they are flat, 1 minute to rip it out and replace it.
But I have extremely mediocre results there. I can't teach anybody anything.

Now let's come to the questionable shit.
The so-called fuckin 'stolen shit.'

* The bike Igor is examining was brought in by this fellow. It has long been a Toronto legend that Igor ran a gang of these guys; that he was Fagin to an army of marauding bike thieves. Whether or not this is true, he called them his Providers.

But nobody wants to do anything.
They just want to point out that I buy hot shit.
The bikes come off the street and surprisingly low percentage gets dealt with by the cops.
Now if you are actually ready to do something, then I'm eager to assist you in curbing the issue.

Right now, between us, if you are a bicycle thief you have very safe business going on. Very safe business.
So like for the last few years, I've been yelling at the cops. They are just used to getting large piles of money with their salaries and benefits, while Public suffers.
Everything is documented, so then the cops can grab the whole gallery of misfits dumping their shit. If they want to.
I keep tormenting these people. Each of these people. They are profiled. They are written in the book.
ID.
Address.
Everything.

VOLUNTEER
These are ground-floor people. IQ of 90 or less. Bank account of zero or less.
I say to Providers: 'I'm not a cop, but the cops will have a very good look at you.'
*
But I've learned that cops and Business Community does not have any ambition to work on the matter.

* In the eyes of the law, this transaction is legal, however shady it may be. It doesn't matter where the bike came from as long as the seller is willing to sign the ledger, and Igor doesn't resell it within the 3-week waiting period.

You see, Business Community does not appreciate stopping bike thieves. You can't have fuckin crazy cops running around charging everybody for their crimes.
We need crooks. Integral part of Business Community.
Fuck, more than integral.
Fuckin skeletal. Skeletal.
Of course it's clear. If everybody is happy, that's no good for business.
You have to keep people on their toes. Thieves stealing shit.
Business Community wants you in the dark.
So you keep your plastic outside and keep purchasing and purchasing.
Why wouldn't you fix shit so that it doesn't break anymore? But that's a blind alley. There's no money in that.

But I'M the crook?
I leave bikes outside the same day that they come.
I leave them outside, even though I'm the biggest fuckin thief in western hemisphere.
So sometimes people come and look and go, all excited, 'Oh that's my fuckin bike.'
I go, 'Yeah that's why it's fuckin here. So that you can find it.'
It's a fuckin insult. For shit like this I don't have time to waste, but if you think I'm a crook and you want to evaluate?

Well, fuck you.
You know where
to find me.

CHAPTER 6:
I'M ENTERTAINED. NOW, ENTERTAIN ME FURTHER

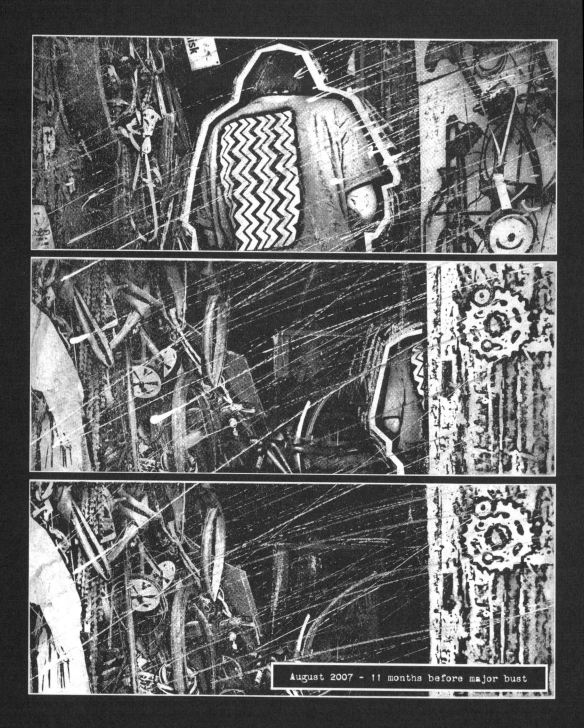

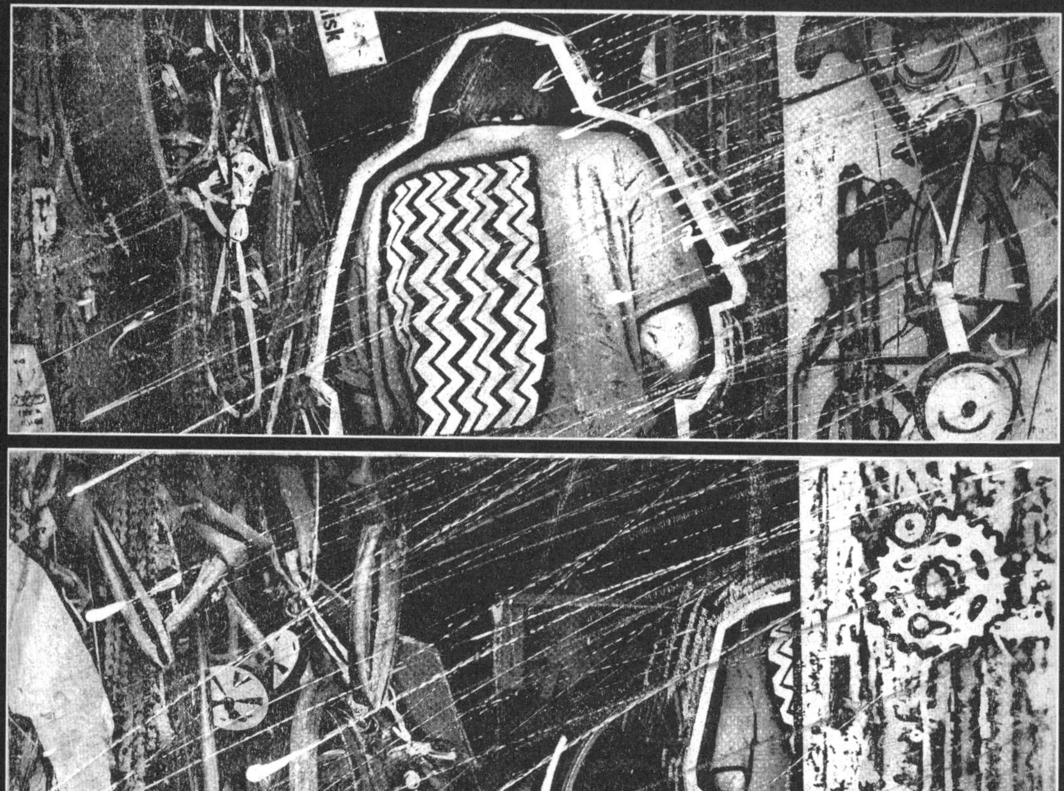
August 2007 - 11 months before major bust

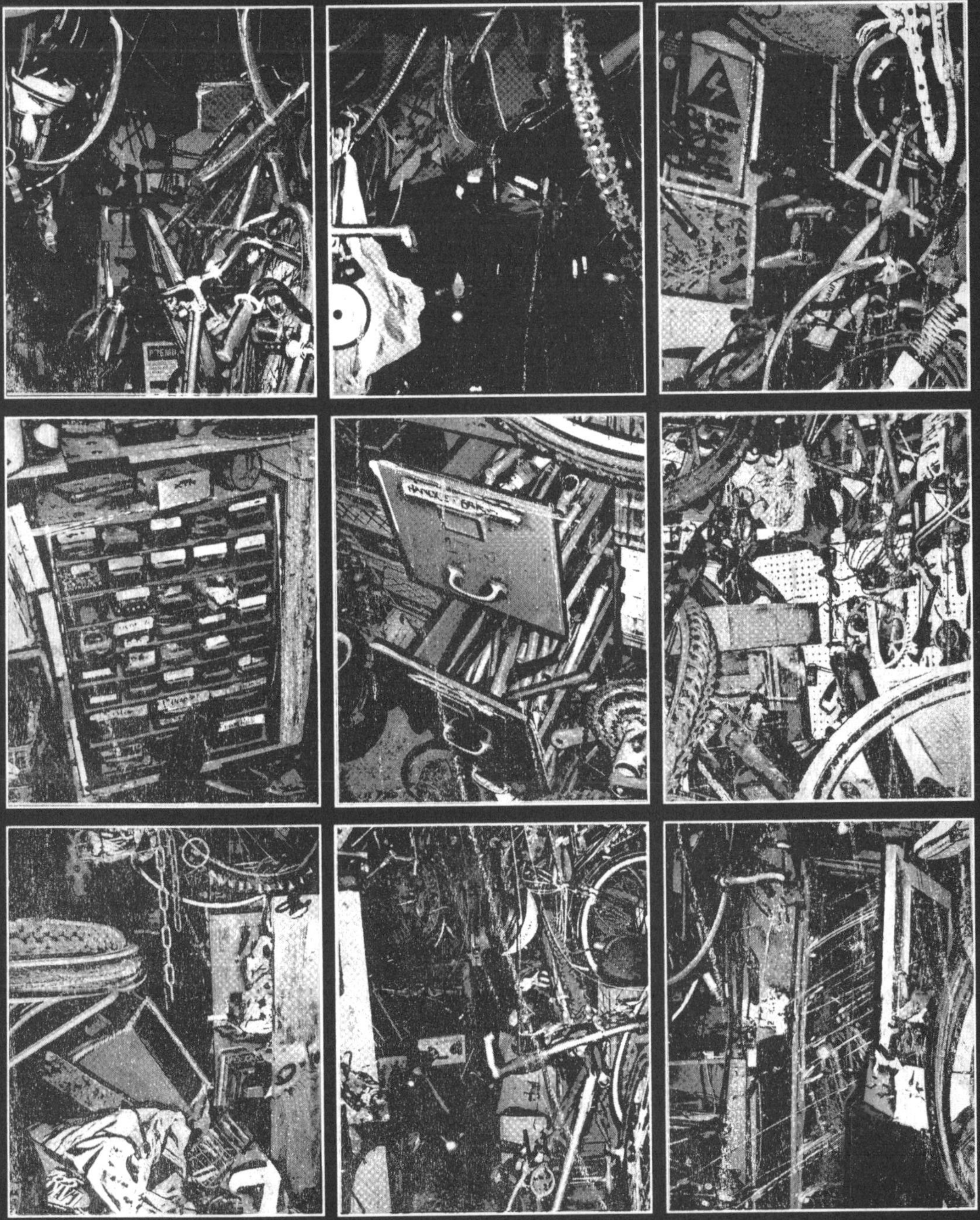

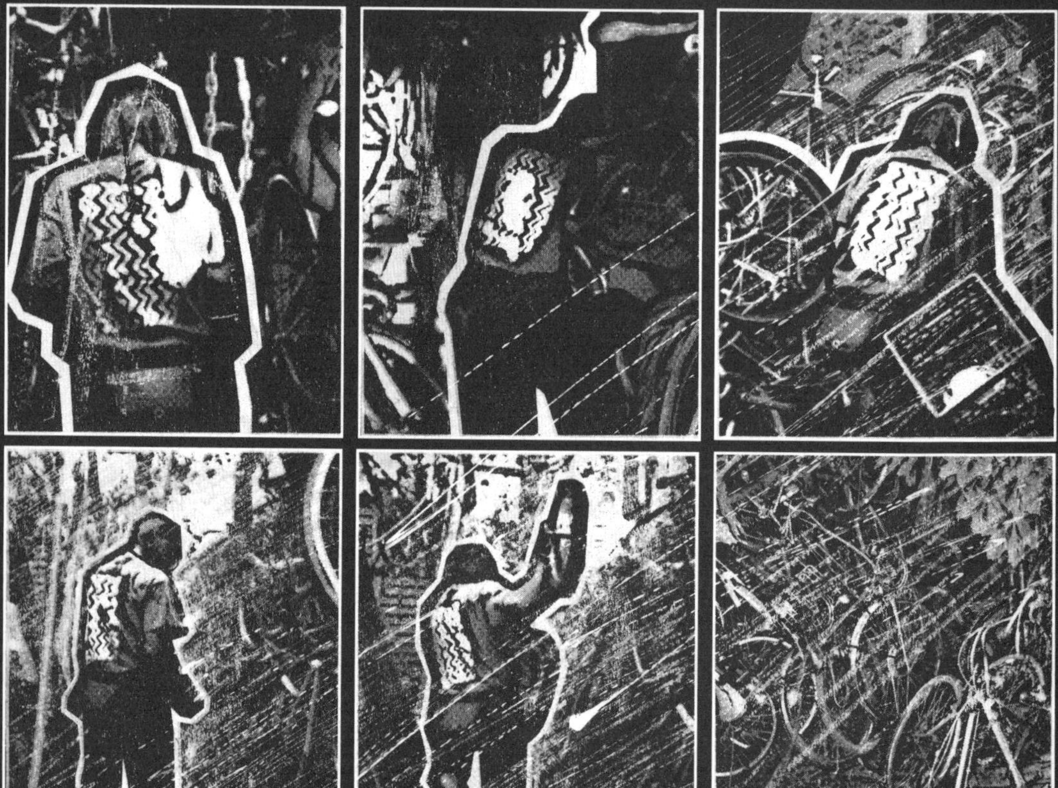

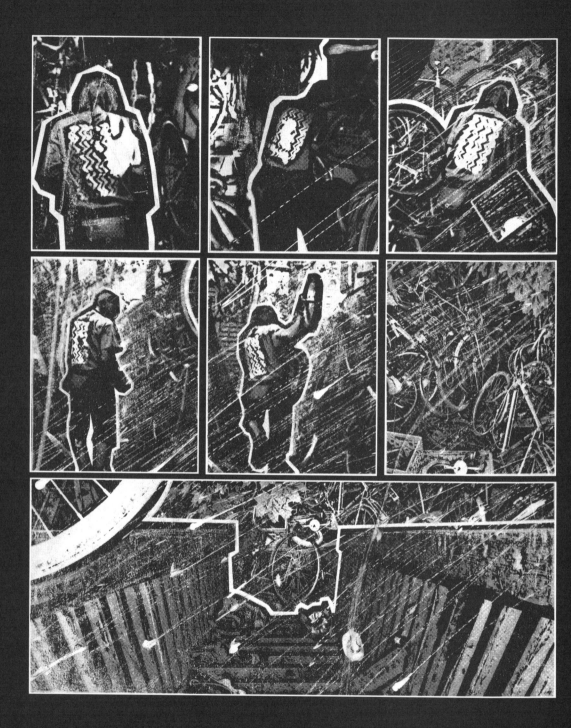

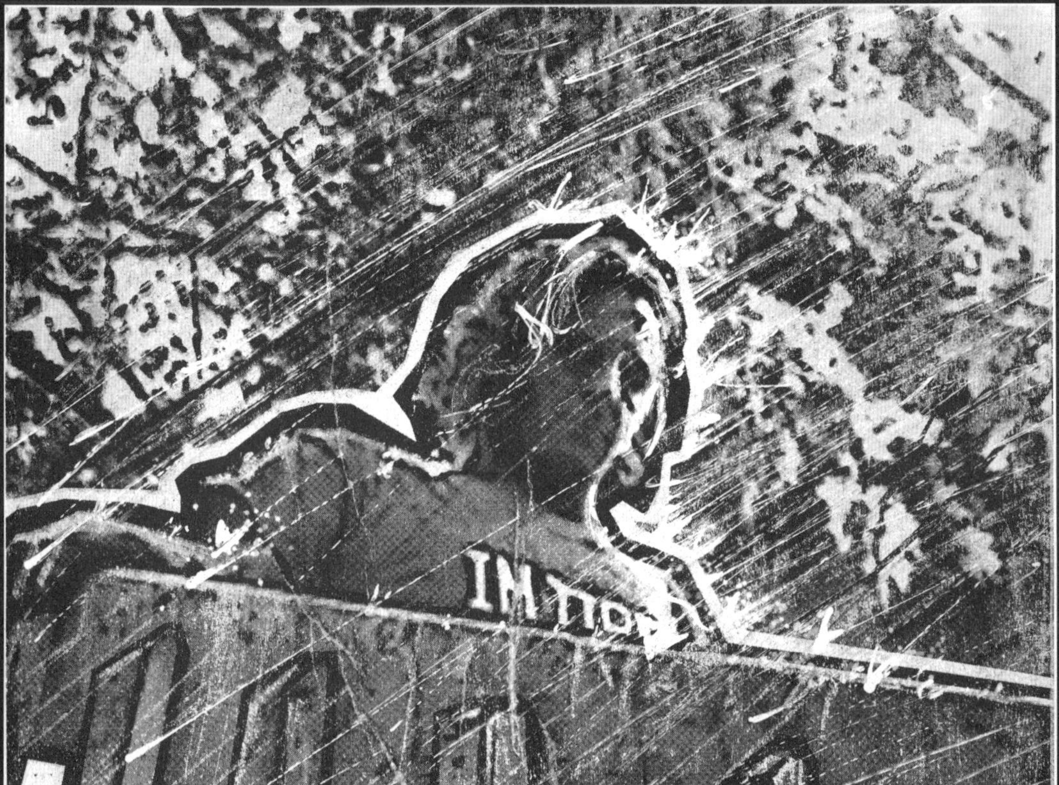
clang
crash

clang
ting
Free training.
Free obstacle training.
To evolve coordination. Ha ha!
At the same time, making job fairly hard.

The question is not what's where. The question is what Public wants.
The thing is, Public does not know what they want.
ka-rash
Generally, I find everything. I know where is everything.
If dude comes in, and he says, 'There! That's my bike over there!'
I say, 'Very well, very well. I'm entertained. Now, entertain me further.'
So, I interview him or whatever.
'Tell me, are there any differences on the bike? What? It's all the same? Oh, okay.'
Then, I'm facing him with the data.

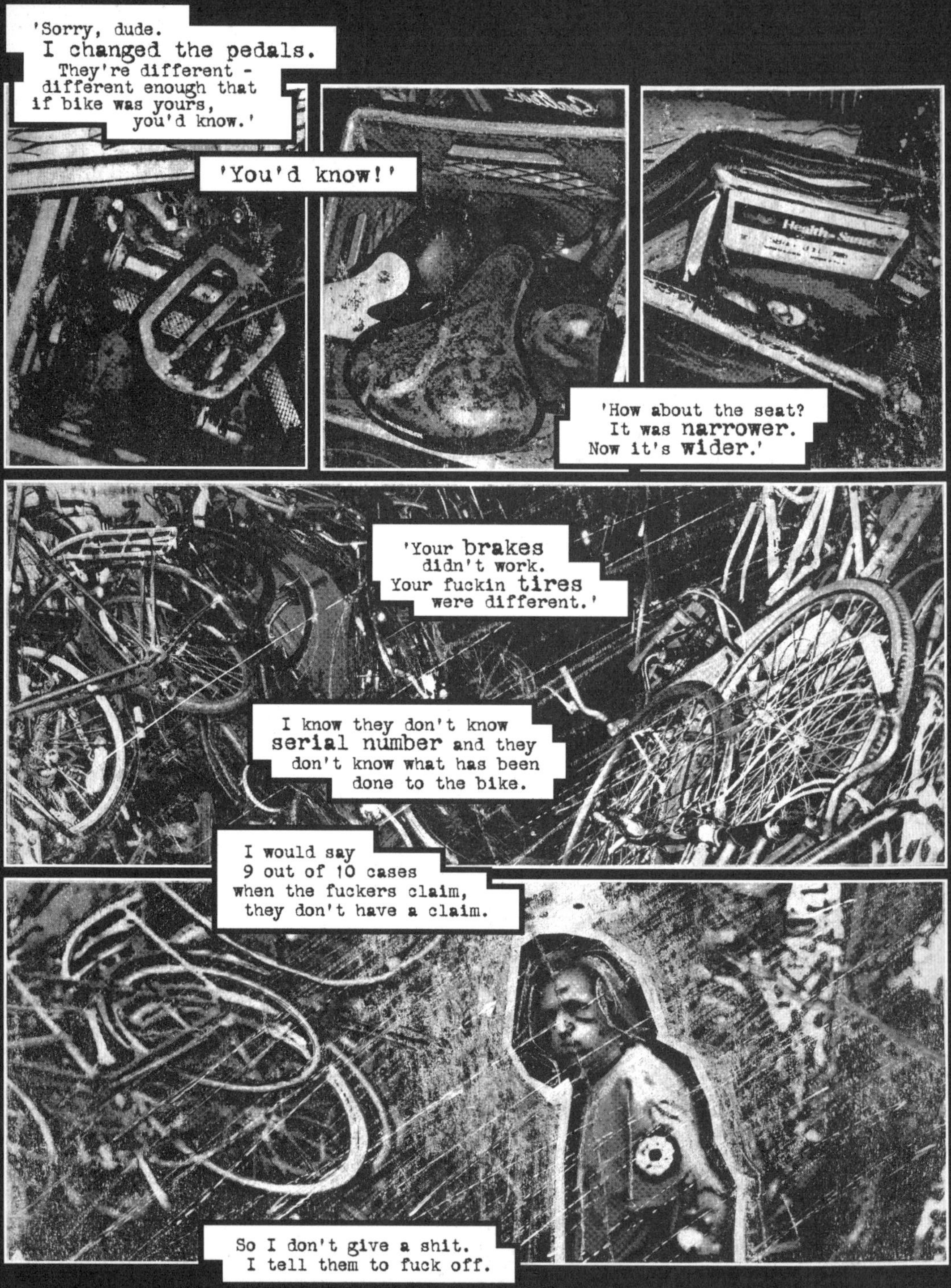
'Sorry, dude.
I changed the pedals.
They're different -
different enough that
if bike was yours,
you'd know.'
'You'd know!'
'How about the seat?
It was narrower.
Now it's wider.'
'Your brakes
didn't work.
Your fuckin tires
were different.'
I know they don't know
serial number and they
don't know what has been
done to the bike.
I would say
9 out of 10 cases
when the fuckers claim,
they don't have a claim.
So I don't give a shit.
I tell them to fuck off.

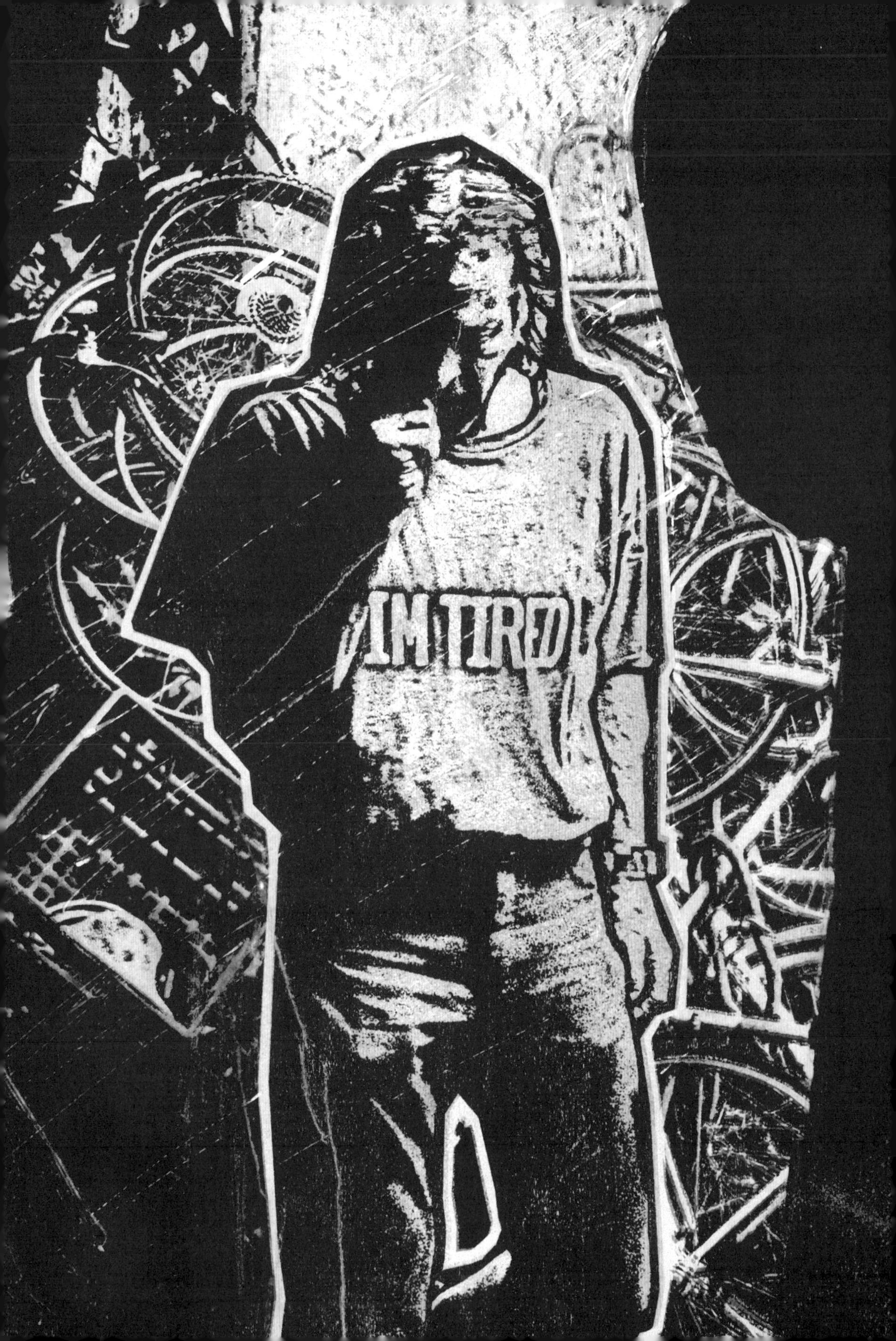
IM TIRED

That's why I bring
my Dogs in.

They're kinder than I am.

I tell them,
'Why don't you deal with the losers.'

I say,
'They're lonely and retarded.'

'They know nothing about anything.
You know nothing about anything.'

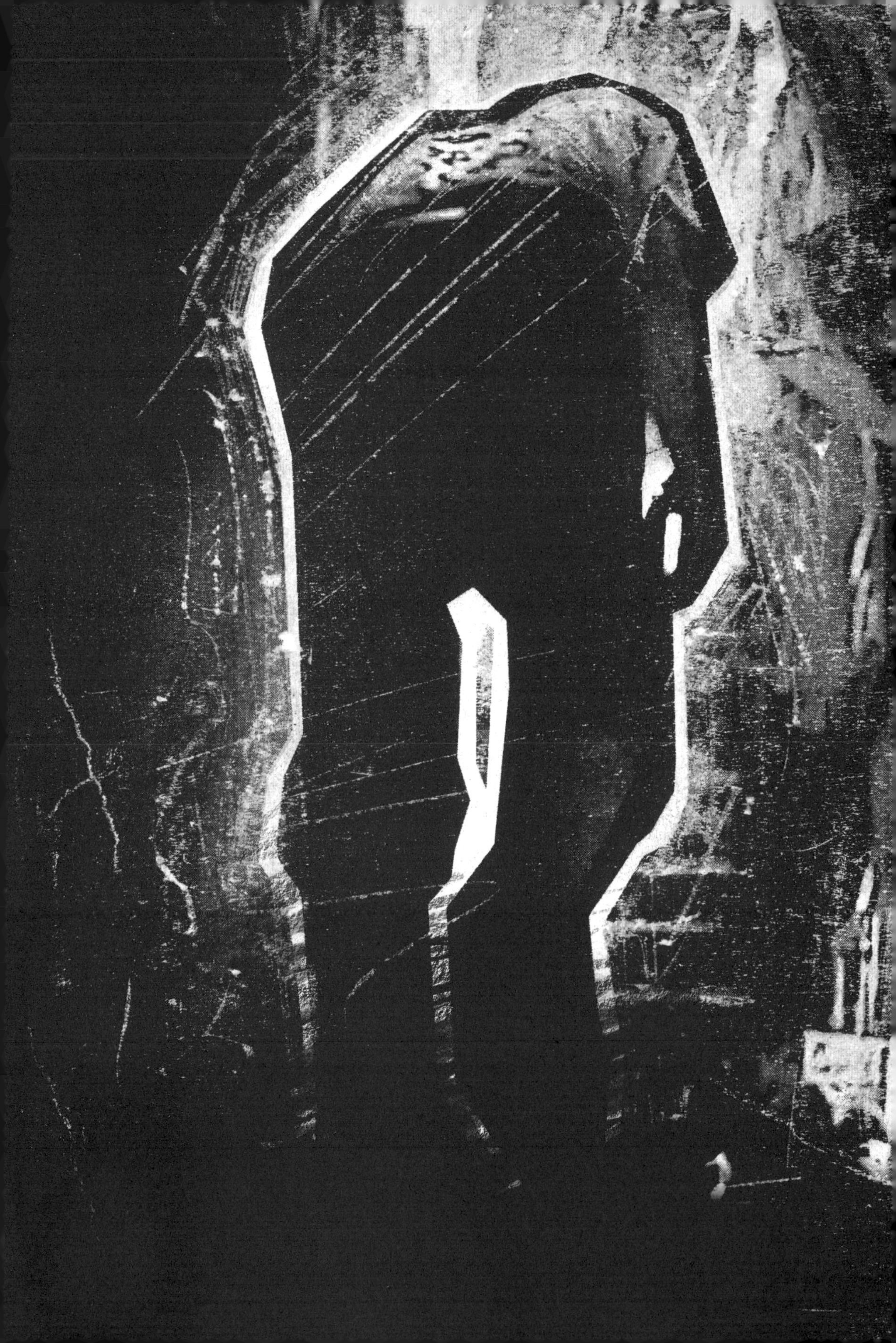

...Hmmm...
I think the thing to do is to make a list - a list of where the shit is.
Oh, the window is closed...
Maybe open it to have less, um, choking.
I kind of let my Dogs... like all my people attempting to build their skills? I call them my Dogs.
So my Dogs live here.
When they are in the minus. When they are in perpetual bleeding mode.
Dogs just come and ask for job. Or I put like, 'Help Needed - Part Time.'
They all claim, 'Oh I know it all.' But as soon as they open their fuckin mouth they get ahead of themselves.
I have very mixed feelings about these Dogs, because losers like this need to be around constructive people that may invest in them.
So, I invest in them...
Shit. We got something... going on here. That was the fantastic professional job. 25 years' warranty on the roof.
Started leaking like 2 years after.

What to do? It's a free country right?
Clearly I didn't break my piggybank buying these records. They are mostly from garage sales.
As everything else...things have been... things are declined by other people. These are the only things worth owning.
These poor records... they are not really in fantastic shape.
This mess was from one of my Dogs.
Best job he could muster was to just throw bikes around.

A FIELD GUIDE TO THE U.S. ECONOM
%
And now the basement.
IM TIRED
That's seriously high Monkey Factor, the basement.
*
TIRED

* For a proper disquisition on "Monkey Factor" - Igor's interpretation of social Darwinism - please flip forward to your own complimentary cut-out page at the end of Chapter 8.

Facility of 'stolen goods.'
The basement...

Stolen markers, stolen everything else.
Stolen receipt book...
Let's see. What else did I manage to steal here?
Stolen, mangled 2-inch tubes...
There you go. My stolen pen works...
Bee-yoo-tiful! Stolen white glove and more tubes...
Grip shift. Grip shift. Grip shift...
Obviously stolen. Fuckin heat is just beaming off of it.
Wicked shit man! A hot fuckin comb.
Smoking! Ha ha!

ba-ba-ba-bump-
a-bump-a-bum-bum...

Jesus...

But everything is hot
until it's proven it's not,
right?

That's what cops charged me with in 93.
Everything stolen.
They weren't in a big hurry to find one single person to point out and say, 'That is mine.'
That was not necessary.
...I need some awning here...
Our talents - our talents for dealing with stolen shit are limited.

Hmmm...
What do you think?
Do you think this shirt
is something to keep?
Yup.
This one? This one... good fibres!
We can lose it maybe...
...Maybe not.
This towel doesn't seem to be
the freshest...

MOTHER
BATES & DODD
Budweiser

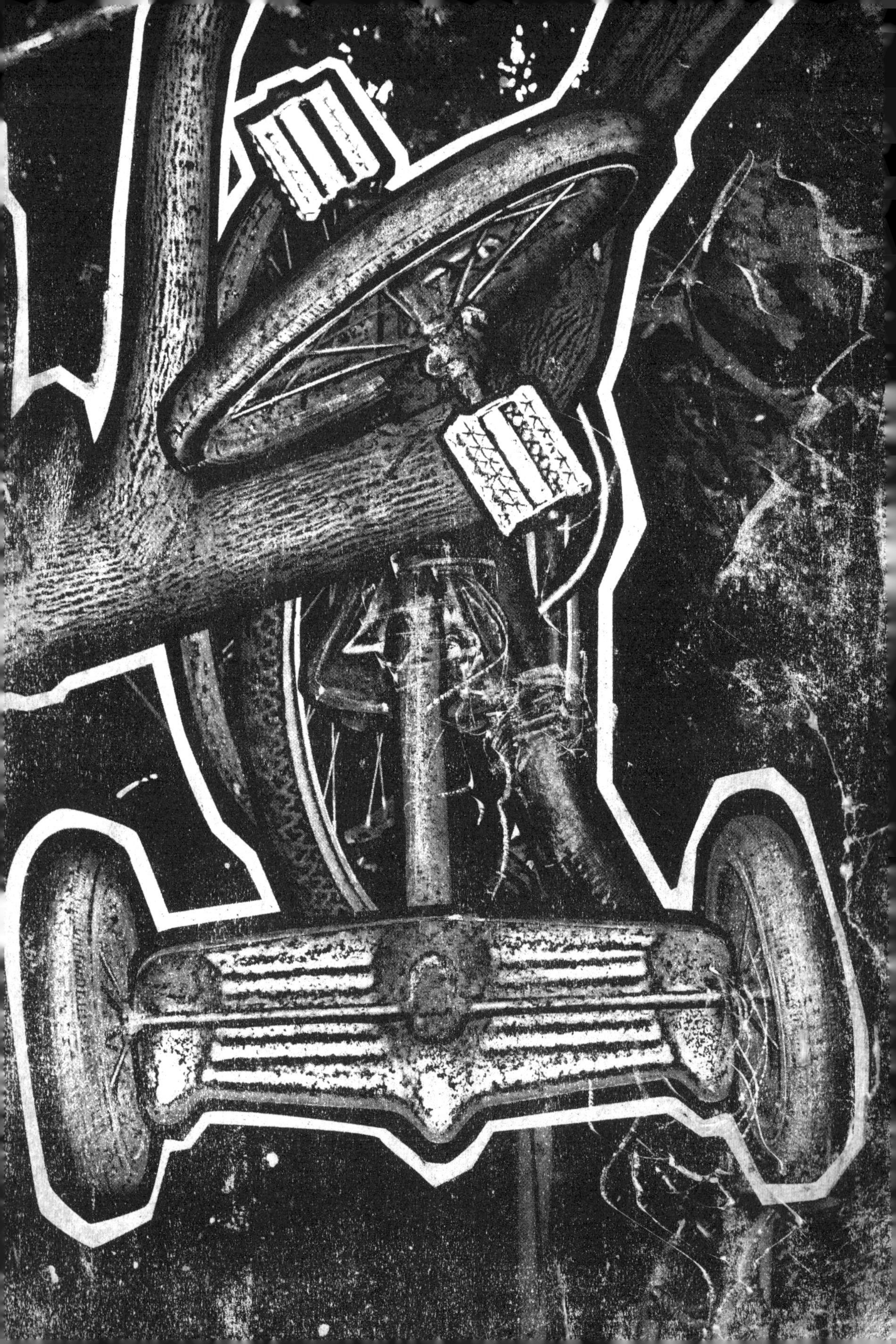

PART III

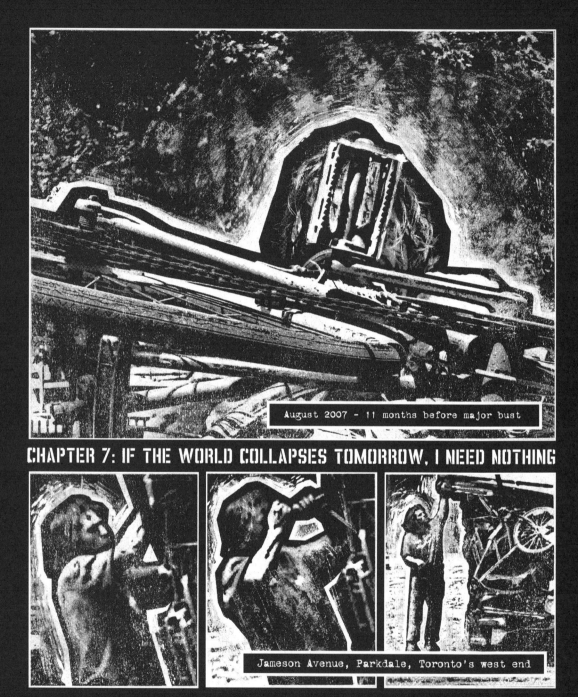

August 2007 - 11 months before major bust

CHAPTER 7: IF THE WORLD COLLAPSES TOMORROW, I NEED NOTHING

Jameson Avenue, Parkdale, Toronto's west end

Lake Shore
Boulevard,
Toronto
Okay,
we need to
get to Dundas and
Jane Street inside
10 fuckin minutes here.
Scrapyard closes at noon.
Pretty near impossible.
Impossible combined with
looking for trouble.
Even if they let me take
some of this shit off...
Oh fuck.

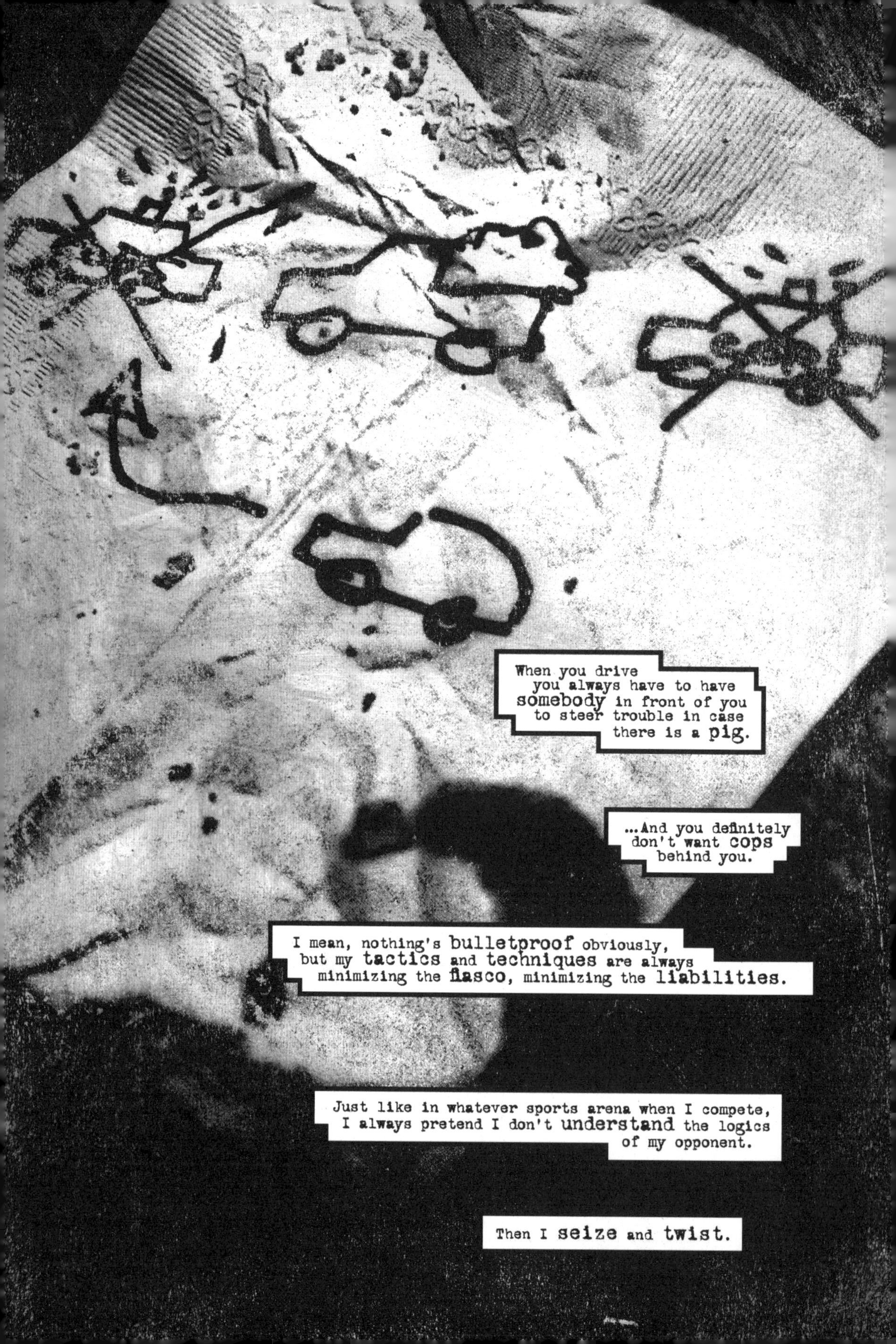
When you drive you always have to have somebody in front of you to steer trouble in case there is a pig.
...And you definitely don't want cops behind you.
I mean, nothing's bulletproof obviously, but my tactics and techniques are always minimizing the fiasco, minimizing the liabilities.
Just like in whatever sports arena when I compete, I always pretend I don't understand the logics of my opponent.
Then I seize and twist.

11:55
Fuck, we're doing well.
Igor drives by a wedding party...
Ahhhhh!
ST. CECILIA'S
CATHOLIC CHURCH
Someone's getting stiffed!
!
!
This is such a waste!
Such a stupid thing!
Meanwhile, we've got like a James Bond race here, with 25 bucks worth of shit scrap.
6502
C'mon fat-ass, let's keep moving!

Yes!
It's extremely lovely
that in these circumstances
I made it.
!
look at
this here!
holy crap!
ah, fuck!
you want
everything off?
Nah, nah.
Just metal.
i close at
12 o'clock...
so, get it
off quickly.

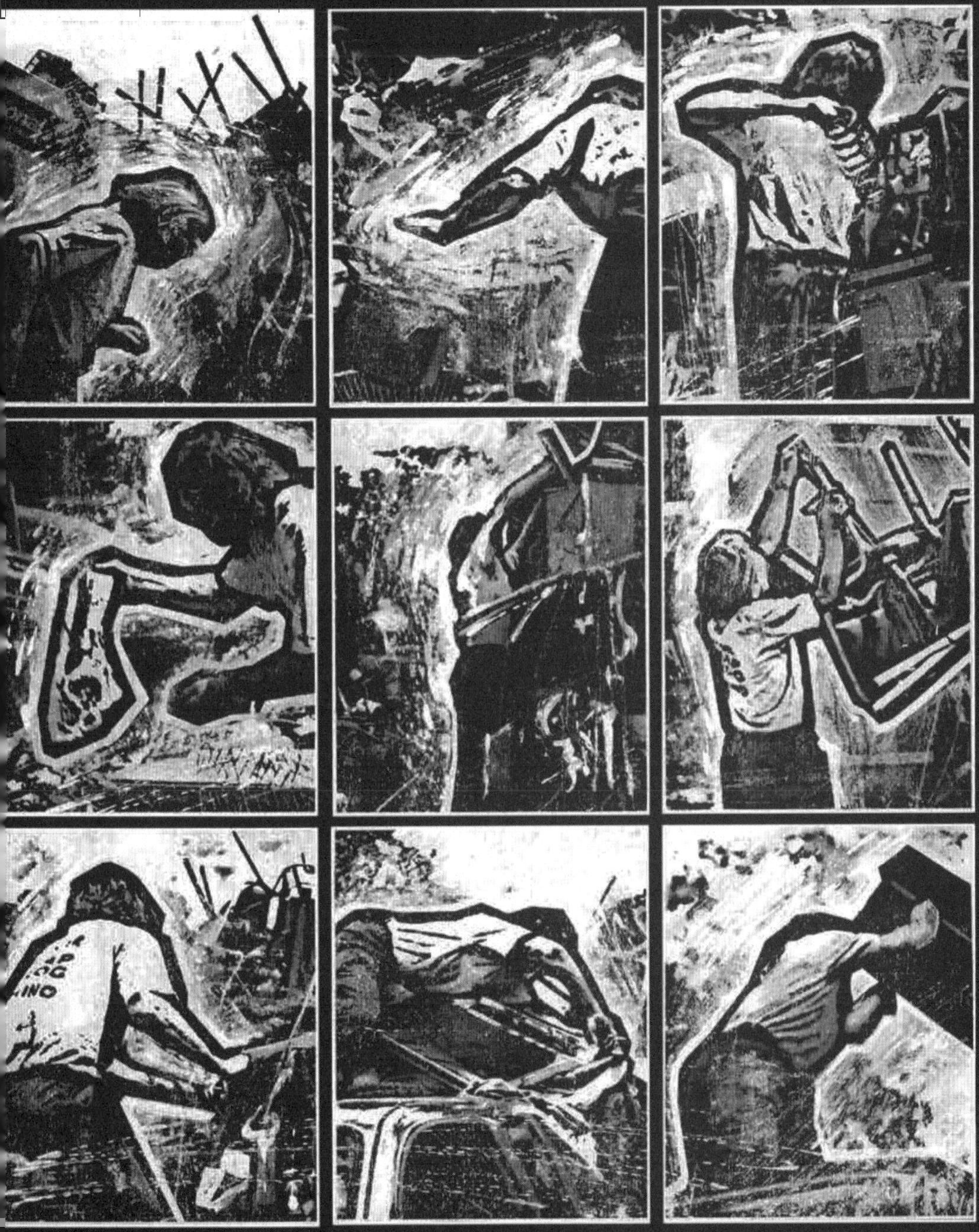

?
!
sk-kkkr-heek
CRRRRASHHH

?
!
?
breep
Nah - give me a
call in a little while.
I'm not at the shop.
NE AR
LEAF
FROO
RHINO

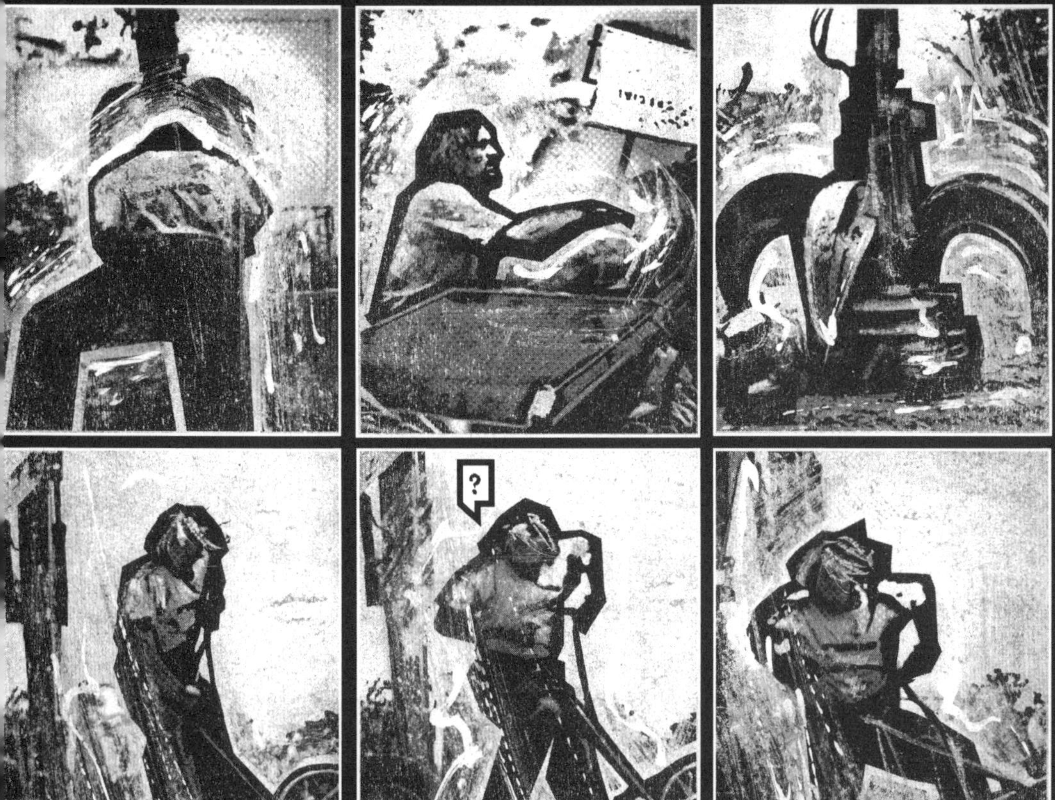
?
Oof!

swiff
swiff
swiff
Minutes later...
Kenk.
K-E-N-K
This is a shitload of
pricey stuff I brought.

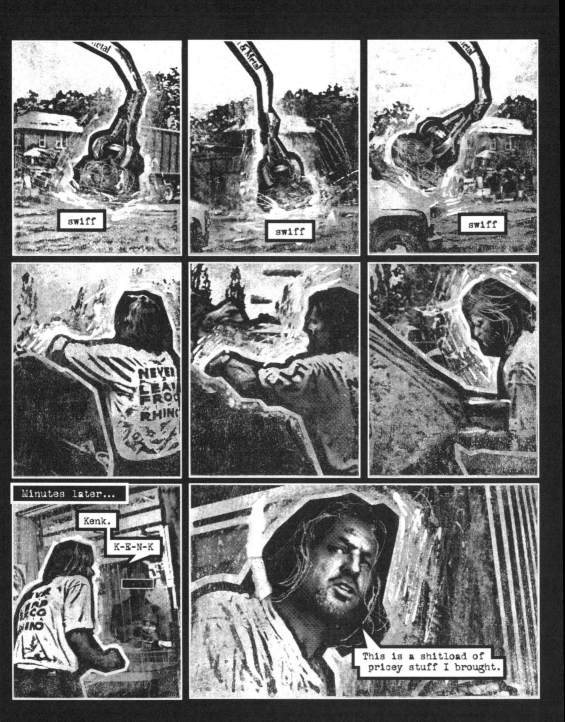

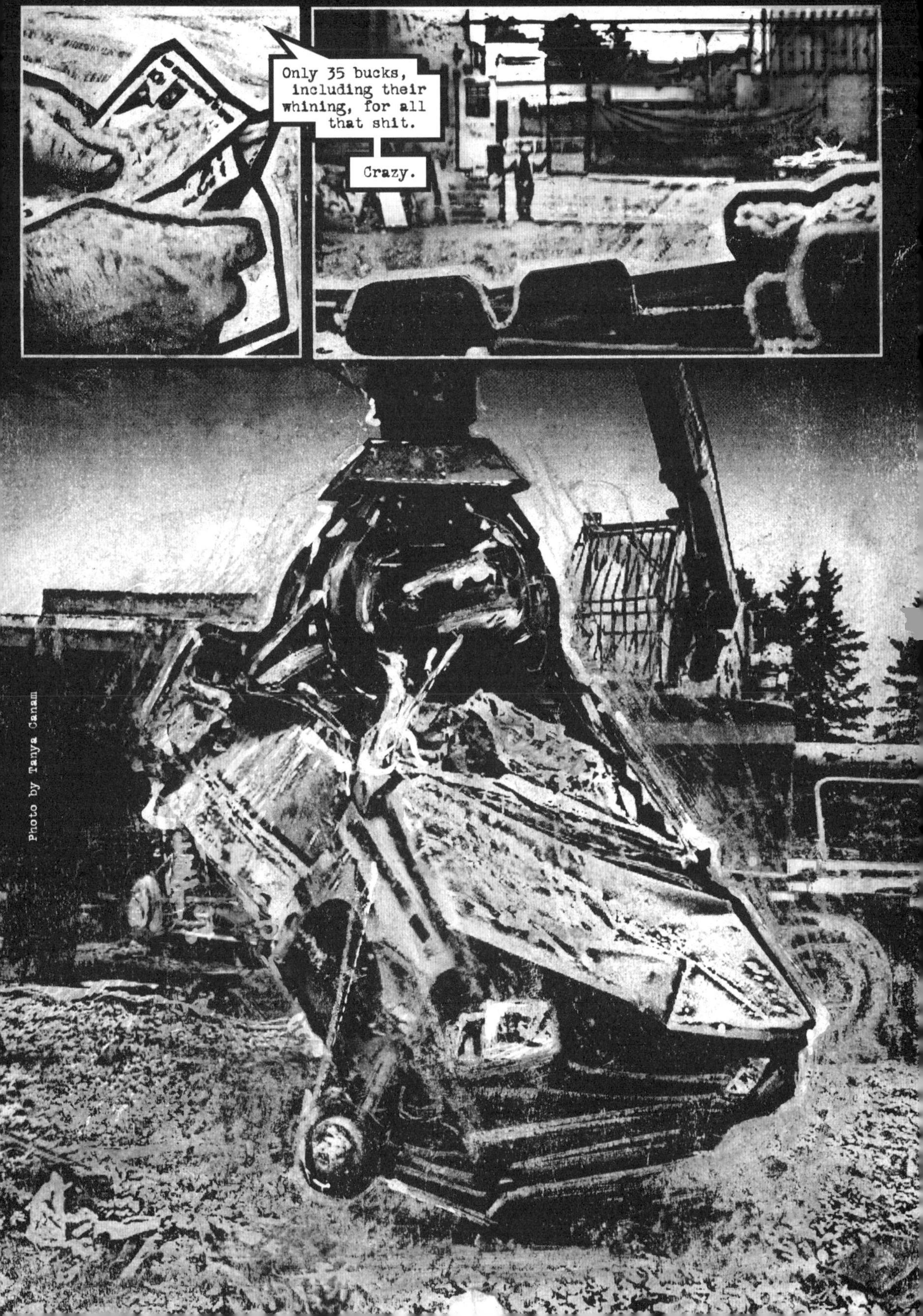
Only 35 bucks, including their whining, for all that shit.
Crazy.
Photo by Tanya Canam

So this month I'm going to be earning - that's before damages on the truck and gasoline and anything else - 1235...1255...
...1255 bucks.
I have to look at what kinds of mileage, but probably I burn $10 worth of gas a day. So that takes down $300, so maybe just under 1000 bucks this month.
Hmm... I think I did hurt my ribs there on the first wipe.
Yeah. It's tough when floor underneath you goes...
Ground underneath you vanishes and you land and there are all kinds of spiky things - chk, chk, chk.

Minutes later...

I'm going to go for the cheapest pizza in the city on this corner.
The jackasses here eat so much pizza it's always hot, always fresh.
And it's $2.25.
Our purchasing power in Canada... it's *IMMENSE*.
Like let's say in Zurich you get half the size of pizza and you pay more than twice as much.
6 bucks for a pizza and this shit is like 3 times the size.
We can buy more by factor of 9!
Toronto
Zurich
You always buy 2 portions, not 1. Because if you buy 2, you pay less tax.
Now, people like me who have travelled extensively, we know that higher buying power does not guarantee a higher level of satisfaction.
Oh, look at that fuckin TV!

sssskkkkrrrrrrrrk

"...budding subprime crisis in the united states housing market hasn't done much to dampen the dow jones, which is approaching an all-time high of 14000..."
Shit.
Unbelievable.
The city is shooting their fuckin feet by putting scrappers like me off the market.
City is in horrendous shape, garbage is massive challenge. There is lack of funds to deal with garbage.
We're not even worried about the imminent gas masks, coming and making things more expensive.
Public are going to have to buy cans of fresh air. It's fantastic! Good for business. Good for fuckin business.
But me, I do not need anything. If the world collapses tomorrow, I need nothing. I can just run my business for years without buying $1 worth of equipment.

[redacted] I need [redacted]

nothing. [redacted]

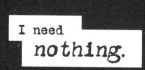

glug
glug
glug

ge against
e machine

Lovers' Interlude

"it was a joke at first."

"it was 2000, i was 30, back from new york city, just finished my doctoral thesis at juilliard. it was a seminal point in my life. i'd rehearsed 8 hours a day for as long as i could remember. it was the beginning of summer and i just wanted to fry my brains and just be stupid."

"he was striking as a person. i went through that store just marvelling and – lo and behold – i noticed a CD of an obscure russian composer. igor went on this amazing rave about contemporary composers – it's all he listens to. the old stuff – brahms, beethoven – is 'stale music.'"

"it turned out he had seen me play at a recital. it all felt a little cheesy, a little fated. we felt that we'd fallen madly in love, but we were mature, with no illusions. we knew that it was doomed to fail."

"it's the age-old story, if you want to look at it that way, of beauty and the beast."

"we're unrelated beings that have just 1 thing in common."

"we feel good together."

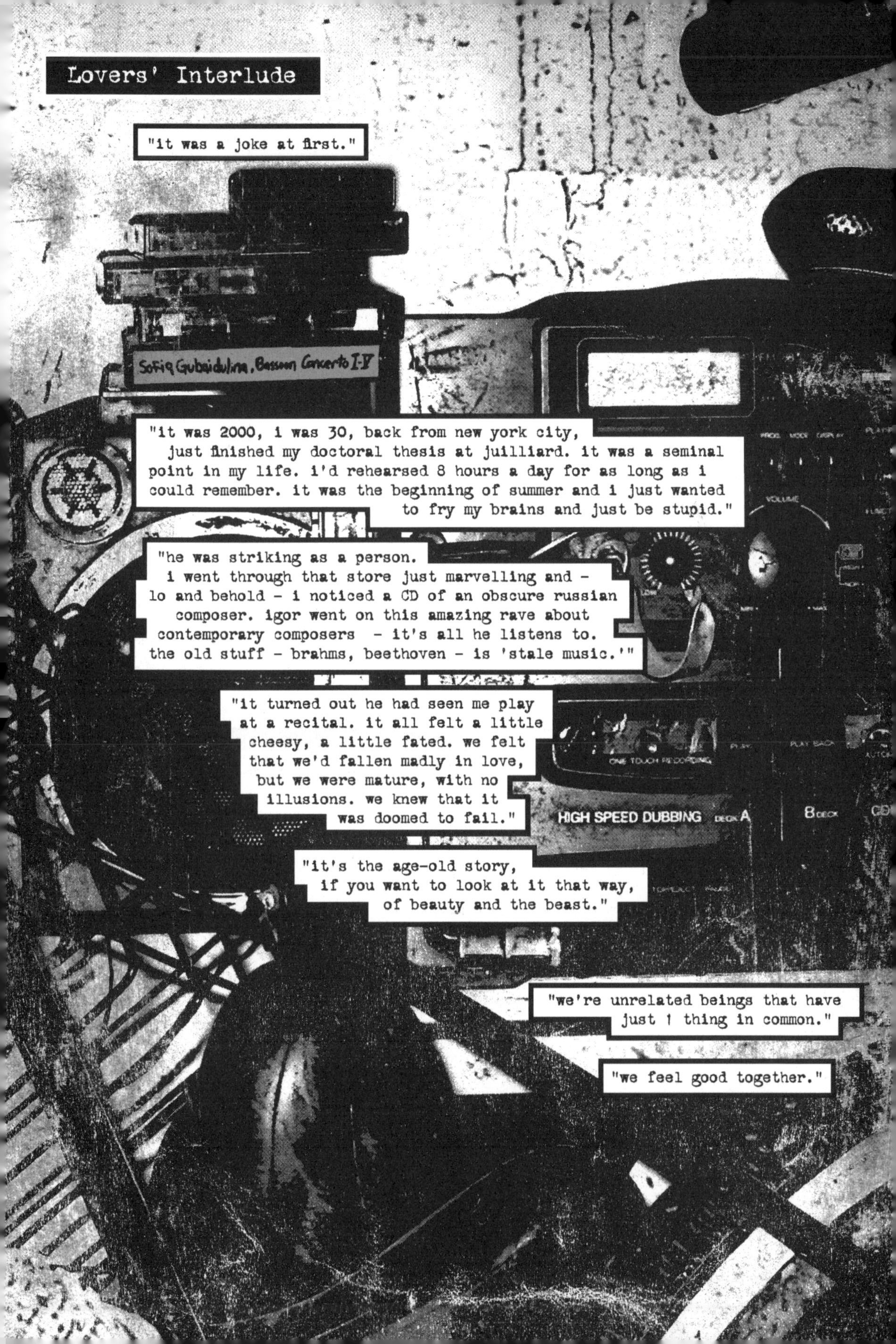

Sofia Gubaidulina, Bassoon Concerto I-V
ONE TOUCH RECORDING
HIGH SPEED DUBBING

"my parents, i can tell you, were not happy."
"i suppose you could say that they're conservative. but igor's a challenge for everybody. outsized, completely rebellious, unconventional. my father always said, 'my instinct is that this person is not good for you.'"
"i didn't care. igor is an untamed person. fascinating. he gives a sense of how his mind works, which is rare in people. he can be confusing. sometimes entertaining. sometimes admirable. you could call him artistic – or autistic – but when his ideas click it is something to behold."
"One of my challenges has been to learn to accept him. when I call him an obsessive recycler, I say that he collects other people's garbage."
"he's convinced it will be used again, that nothing more should be manufactured."
"in this, igor is a person of great ideas and ideals. he just hasn't found a medium for them."
"he's always said, 'you will have such problems because of me. it's up to you how much you're willing to sacrifice.'"
"ultimately, it comes down to the fact that our chemistry holds a very deep affection for each other. we have a very deep bond."
"we're just humans, you see, and we don't want to be alone."

This is Yorkville, Toronto's ritziest shopping neighbourhood - 20 or so blocks northeast of Igor's Bicycle Clinic. In the 1960s it was a shaggy-dog bohemian fantasia, with mixed-race blues bars and jazz clubs standing in contrast to the rest of white, Protestant Toronto. If you'd like to draw a parallel between the transformation of this 'hood and that of Queen Street West some 40 years later, go right ahead.

And this is the rental house Igor has shared with Jeanie Chung since 2002. Miraculously - and despite numerous complaints by neighbours about the messy front yard - no one has managed to kick them out.

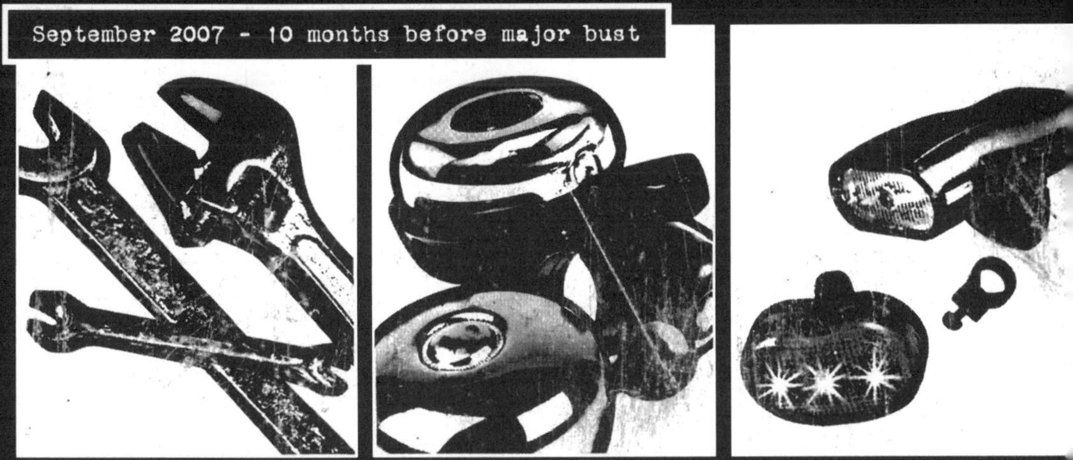
September 2007 - 10 months before major bust

CHAPTER 8: WE ARE ALL A BUNCH OF DEPRESSIVE CRAPPERS

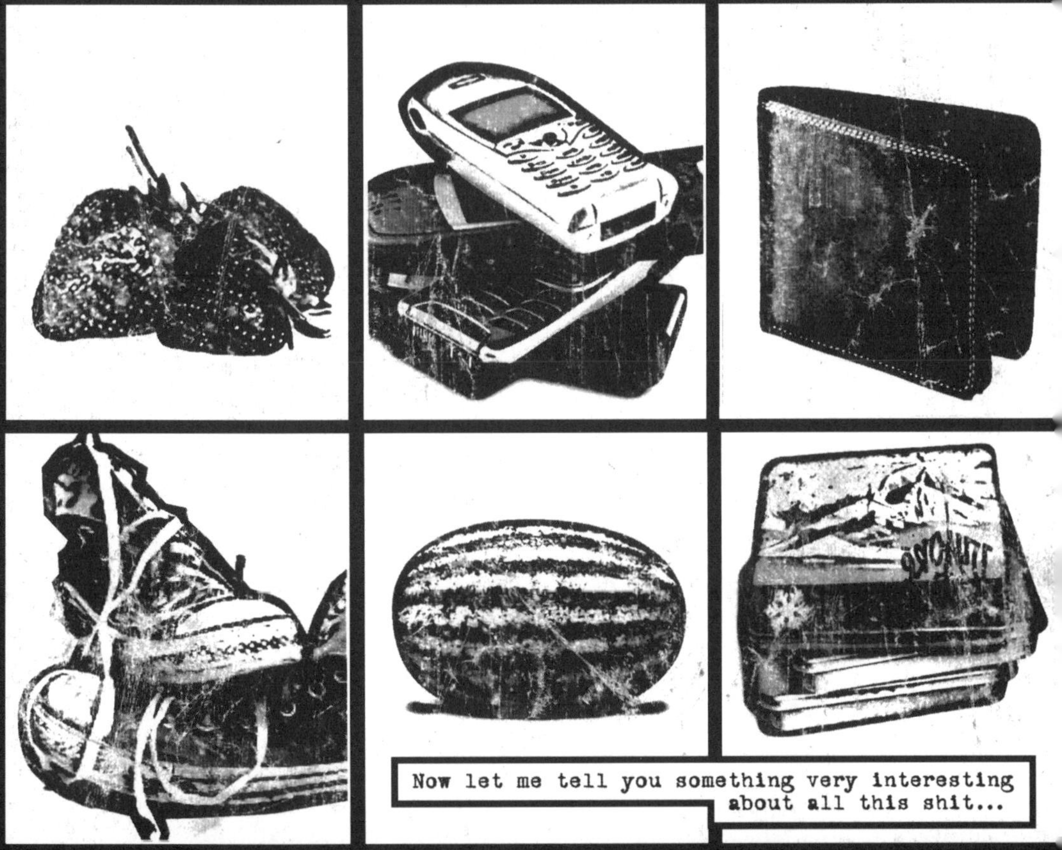
Now let me tell you something very interesting about all this shit...

Almost every time at Moss Park, I find something for crazy cheap - shoes, tools, cellphone, even food.
They give you a big fuckin bag of food for 5 bucks.
Bicycles, everything.
I mean it's not just odds and ends. It's not just garbage. Some serious stuff is ending up there.
I can't even imagine or understand how this is possible.
Clearly break-in situations.
Shit like this...
which is clearly...
I feel kind of guilty over this stuff.
Clearly someone lost this shit.
...It's lights and bells and whistles. Bike parts.
you mean they just lifted it off bicycles?
Well, the way I can see is...
The whole whack of them are going around and grabbing anything they can get their sights on.

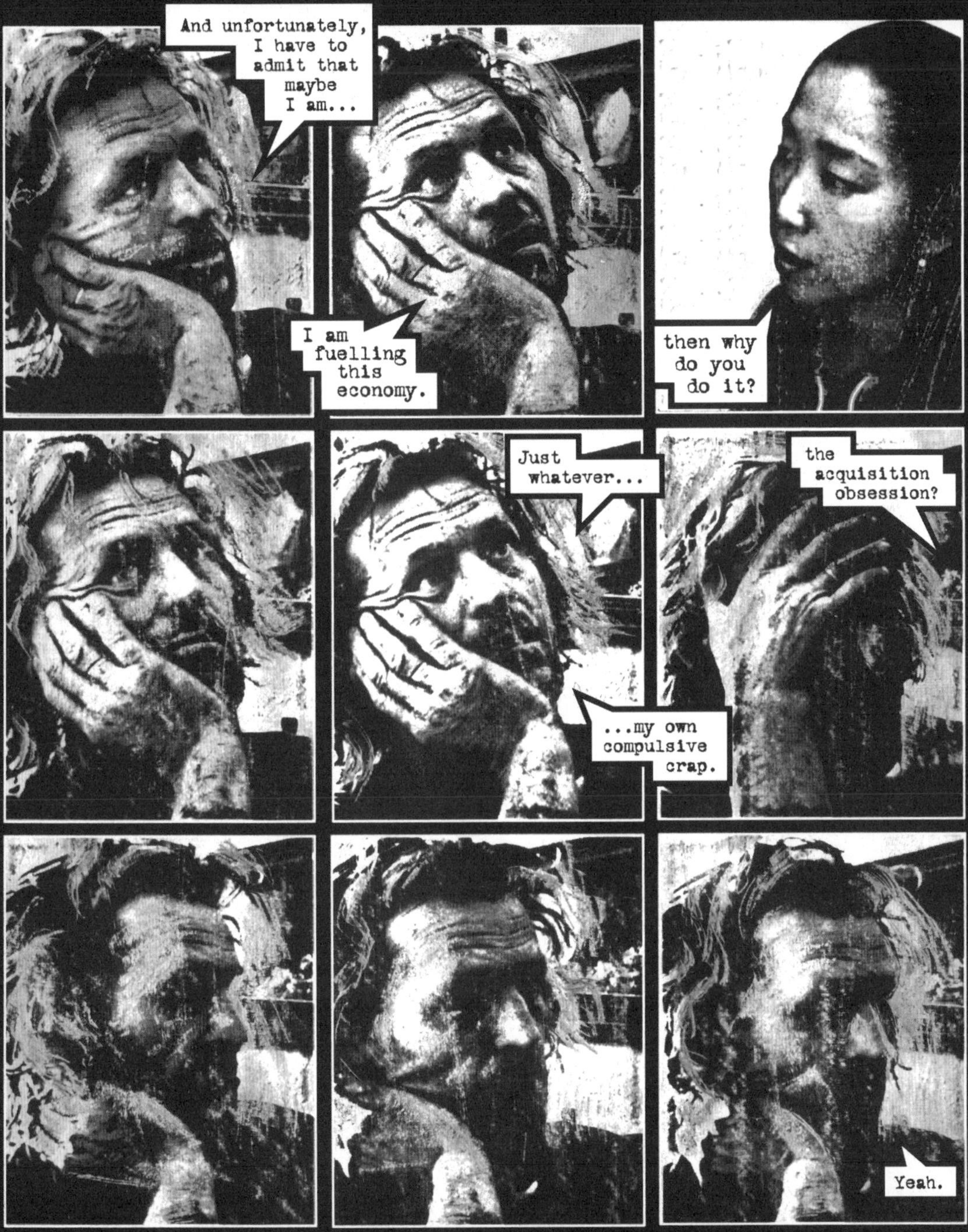
And unfortunately, I have to admit that maybe I am...
I am fuelling this economy.
then why do you do it?
Just whatever...
...my own compulsive crap.
the acquisition obsession?
Yeah.

It was always my plan to collect stuff...
...stuff that's not prone to time factor.
Like all this shit here.
This was my loot today.
I got like 3 boxes.
3 boxes for 3 bucks.
I collect these things.
I don't know where I get this bug, but I have a bug of wanting boxes.
I collect many things...
I don't buy anything new.
This pants are from garage sale.
The question is whether I feel guilty or not.
I'm having trouble understanding where does it begin and where does it end.

Minutes later, in the kitchen...

tssss
I'm coming from a place where...
stuff that is lying in garbage here was completely and utterly out of reach to me, even though I was far from the bottom of society.
Even if I had the money, I would not have been able to go and purchase stuff. We had absolute rules there.
wait, igor...
are those women's pants?
So? Am I supposed to care?

Anyway, it's painful. It's really painful. At least I don't shove myself with huge liability as the losers do. But it's all wrong. All this insane consumerism.
We're all a bunch of depressive crappers. Our creativity is dying. We are just teeny little cogs.
Let's say what I do - it's all very modest shit.
I'm just running around trying to pick other people's garbage and put it back into use.
It's a mess. And this is why I think society will eventually get the bill at some point.
Because...
what's right and what's wrong...
it's not promptly delivered.
You put out as much as you can and consume as little as you can. So that it's your pleasure to contribute.
In other words, true communism.

But we are not ready for communism.
In Western world, everyone has everything. As we know, the richer you are the bigger your fuckin eyes become.
Even though, in a natural situation, once you are well fed then your interest for food should decrease.
Like I could consume way more in my life if I wanted to.
I could just insult less and take more.
More money from more people.

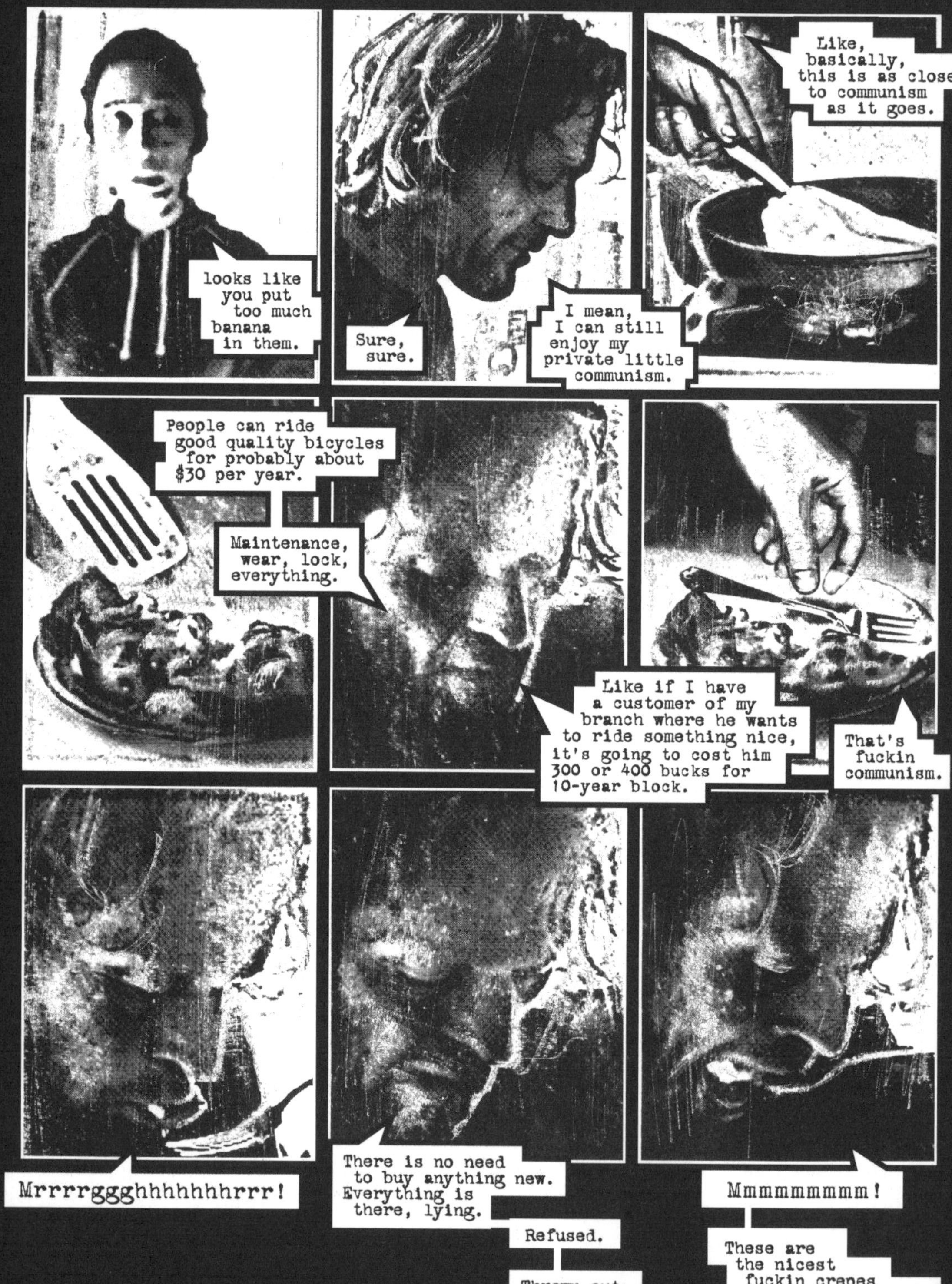
looks like you put too much banana in them.
Sure, sure.
I mean, I can still enjoy my private little communism.
Like, basically, this is as close to communism as it goes.
People can ride good quality bicycles for probably about $30 per year.
Maintenance, wear, lock, everything.
Like if I have a customer of my branch where he wants to ride something nice, it's going to cost him 300 or 400 bucks for 10-year block.
That's fuckin communism.
Mrrrrggghhhhhhhrrr!
There is no need to buy anything new. Everything is there, lying.
Refused.
Thrown out.
Mmmmmmmmm!
These are the nicest fuckin crepes you can picture.

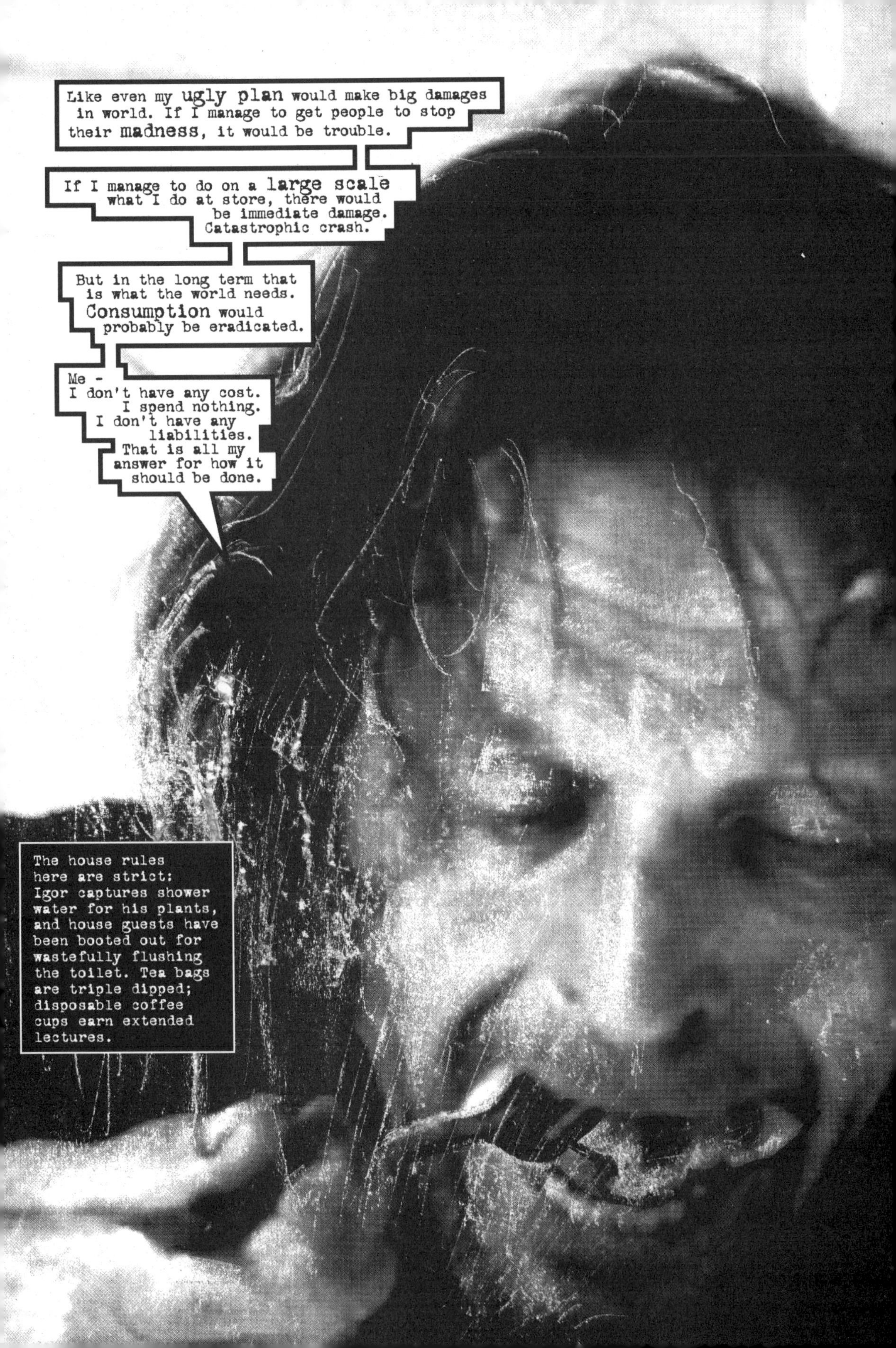
Like even my ugly plan would make big damages in world. If I manage to get people to stop their madness, it would be trouble.
If I manage to do on a large scale what I do at store, there would be immediate damage. Catastrophic crash.
But in the long term that is what the world needs. Consumption would probably be eradicated.
Me - I don't have any cost. I spend nothing. I don't have any liabilities. That is all my answer for how it should be done.
The house rules here are strict: Igor captures shower water for his plants, and house guests have been booted out for wastefully flushing the toilet. Tea bags are triple dipped; disposable coffee cups earn extended lectures.

Dow Jones going fuckin up to the heavens.
Public thinking they're more richer than the next retard.
2007
We'll see.
Apparently 80% of population want to go plastic to look youthful.
There is no fuckin Monkey Factor there.
You've gotta be proud now that you're supposedly mature.
Instead people are fuckin tightening body and rotting inwards fast.
Really bad news.
Anyway, I have another maximum 40 years to shit around, and then that's all there is.
Actually it's pissing me off that this society is demoralizing. They are killing me. Absolutely.
I have been unable, in 19 years, to produce anything. Nothing. I've been kicked in the face, on and on.
Thrown in the court. Thrown in jail. All that shit.
But I don't care.

People do very little.
They sink into this non-productive situations.
Their output is nothing.
They are not excited.
Like I remember I ask my parents, 'Do you like what you do?'
And they say, 'Not really,' and I think, 'Why the fuck are you doing it?'
'Well you know I have to feed you,' and all that shit.
And I say that's bogus.
That's not the right reason to do something.
So at least I would imagine to some extent I am congratulating myself by the fact that I am excited. I am excited and so much so.
Like right now, it's 5:05. I probably lost a couple hundred bucks not being at store a few hours ago. And it's not disturbing me at all.
Like there's no pressure, right?
No worry.
No such thing.

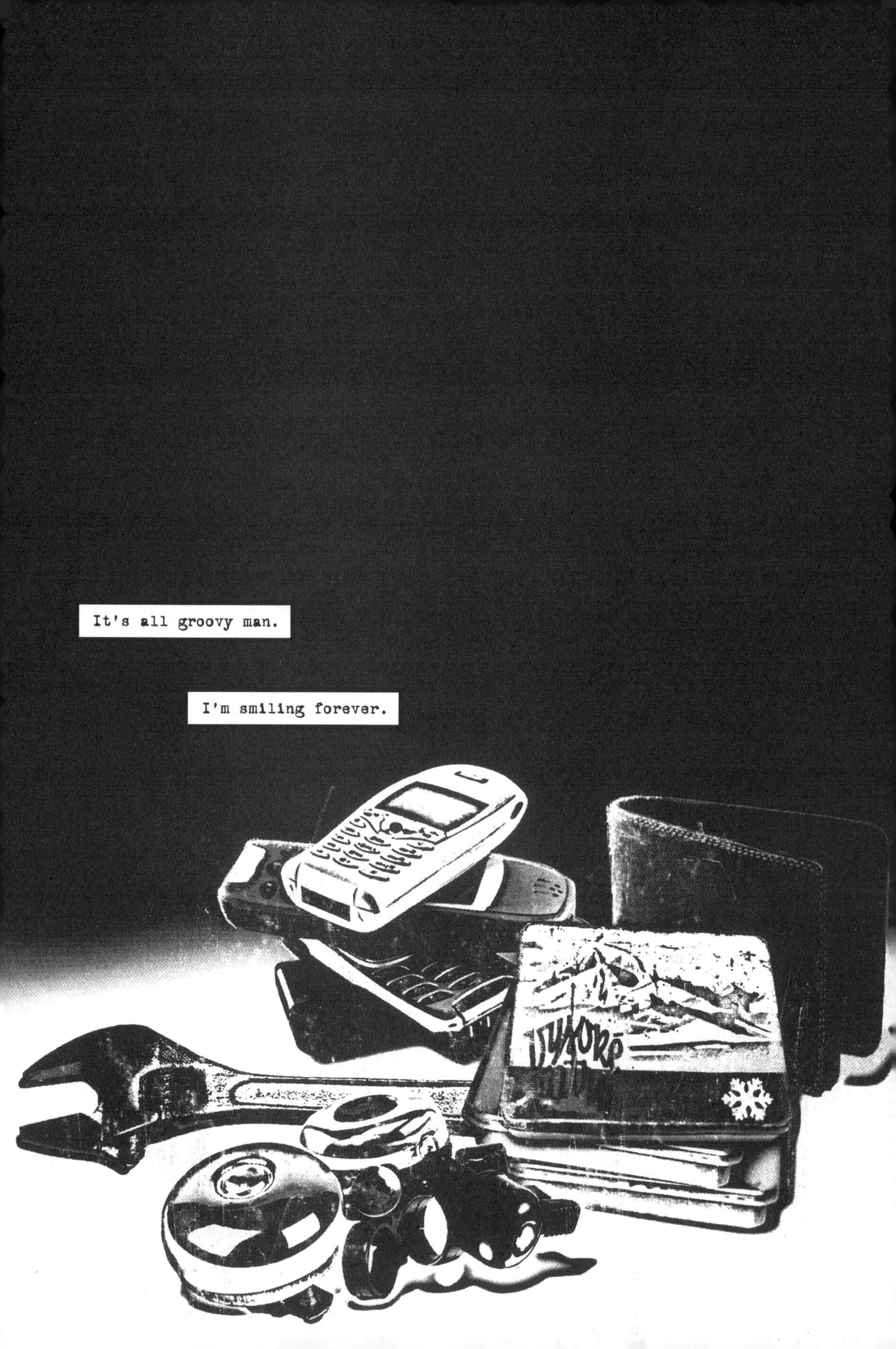
It's all groovy man.
I'm smiling forever.

Monkey Factor

Definition: It's the ability not to crash

So up to couple of hundred years ago, human was just running around and living on a diet of starvation.
But now, we're so opulent. Game is over. We're all a bunch of depressed losers. Toothless. Soft and plush. Monkey Factor is goner. Non-existent.
If you are running around all day long, hustling not to die of starvation, that's the natural path.
Now this shit - this North American shit - is not natural. The shit is going to hit the fan.
The Future of Monkey Factor:
When Chinese really start cranking, right? The Chinese have for the past 30 years been on the verge, the verge of breaking in. So when they crank it up, that's when there's going to be trouble. And Indians, right?
Then you've got 2.5 billion people playing vulgar capitalism. Still got Monkey Factor, but losing it fast.

Photo by Jonathan Ng

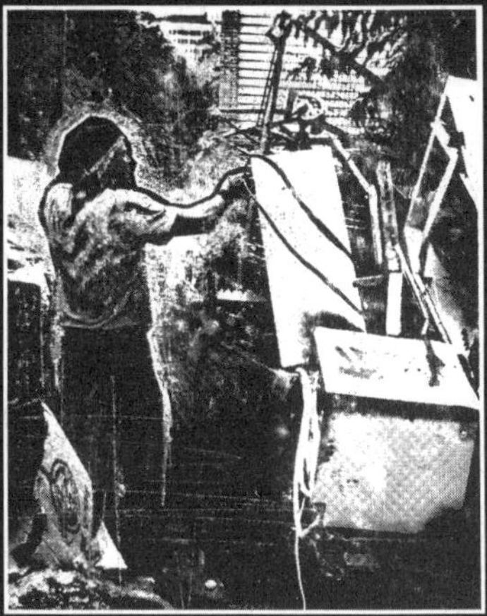

TACOMA
EAGER 1

416 60

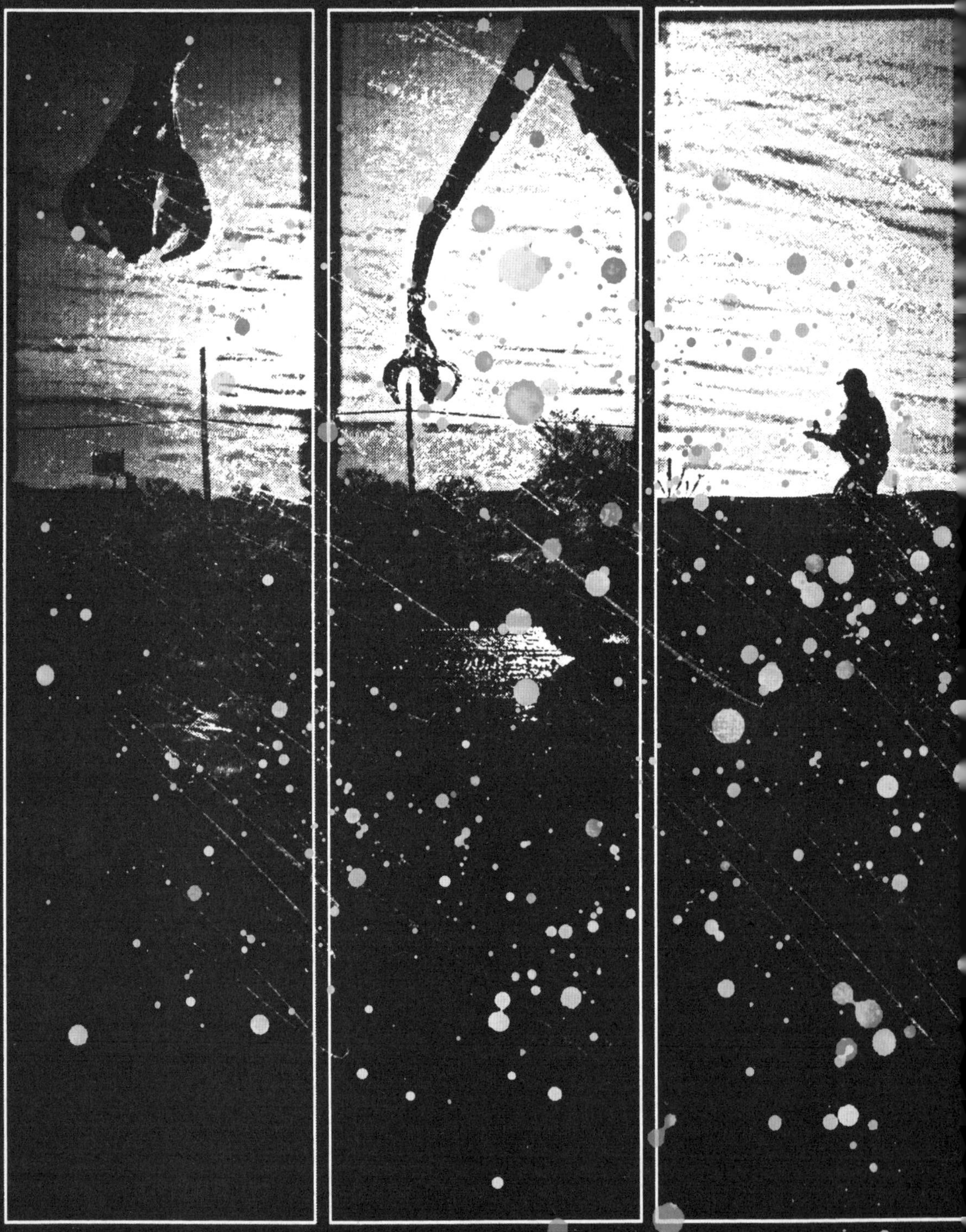

PART IV

The Good News Interlude

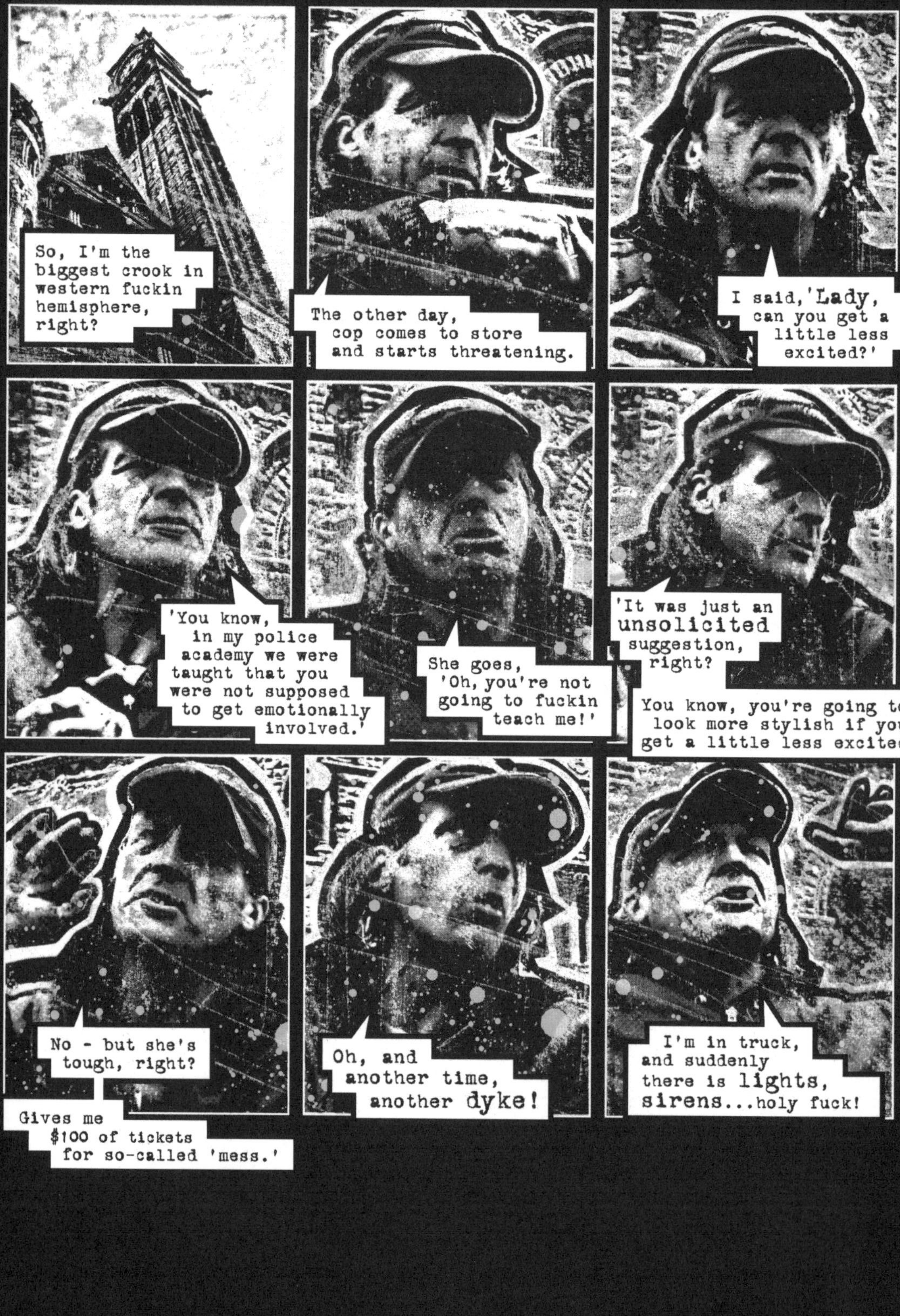
So, I'm the biggest crook in western fuckin hemisphere, right?
The other day, cop comes to store and starts threatening.
I said, 'Lady, can you get a little less excited?'
'You know, in my police academy we were taught that you were not supposed to get emotionally involved.'
She goes, 'Oh, you're not going to fuckin teach me!'
'It was just an unsolicited suggestion, right?
You know, you're going to look more stylish if you get a little less excited.'
No - but she's tough, right?
Gives me $100 of tickets for so-called 'mess.'
Oh, and another time, another dyke!
I'm in truck, and suddenly there is lights, sirens...holy fuck!

I say it's gotta be fuckin western hemisphere totally collapsing right now. Imminent, immediate, and fuckin very catastrophic.
So this bitch is ugly as fuck, right? She is punished.
She says, 'This is an unsafe load.'
Her father and mother were ugly idiots, and now she's idiotic and ugly.
And her punishment is that she's unhappy cop.
So you know, it's a very mild problem for people like me facing this debacle.
...And then another ticket I got yesterday. That was quite irritating.
They rip up my truck, find 7 grams of grass on me. Suddenly it was 8.6 grams even though I only bought 7.
I guess we got very lovely dealers these days, throwing in extra grams. It's fantastic, right?
So that's good news, I guess. Not only is Toronto paradise, but even fuckin dealers are generous.

Photo by Tiffany Maggio

CHAPTER 9:
IN THE NEXT 10 YEARS, I THINK THERE IS A CHANCE THAT I'M GOING TO DIE

March 2008 - 4 months before major bust

This is just ranting and raving, this note I write last night. This is totally unusual for me to write like this in English. I always write in Slovenian because I don't want any cocksucker paying attention to my shit.
Not that they would understand what I'm saying anyway, right?
One of my concerns is that now, like everyone else, I am getting too fuckin poor.
I have to start considering being a little bit more of a whore, making a little bit more money.
Like, we've been losing money all along. So basically I'm a loser, Jeanie is a loser. Everyone is a loser, right? Fuckin not good.

Okay, here goes. "So after 20 years they have turned raging bull into docile chicken, running 80 hours plus a week, and will sell at any minimum hourly rate the output of several people."
"It sounds insane, but I help people ride bicycles for 2 to 50 bucks a year. Nobody ever has or will ever repeat this exercise. Never. It's not doable. Even if they wanted to do it. And nobody wants to because you can't make any money."

Well, the answer to my letter is that I would have to start whoring myself.
I am whoring myself actually. Probably by my standards I'm a cocksucker already.
Because before, when Public ordered bad shit - good for me but bad for them - I would say, 'Okay buddy, I refuse, fuck off.'
They would be totally puzzled. 'Do you not want my money?' And I would say,'Fuck, I'd kill for dough, but not at this price.'
I feel that would be offering my ass to be fucked for dough.
I'm not going to tell you anything new if I assured you that Public is retarded.
I mean, you are retarded if you have all kinds of debts and you still shine with your credit card.
I've met some IQ monsters - very successful people. Yet everybody is on the fuckin verge, right?
Drowning. Water right to their fuckin lips.
And still working to kill themself further, right?

We all know that everything's a fuckin joke, right?
Economy? How rich we are! Like government states 2% inflation. Are you fuckin kidding me? Inflation is 20%.
*
Right now we seem to be getting closer to this threat of collapse or whatever we call it.
Like it won't go that much longer. Like it just cannot go.
There's no road. There's no road now.
There is a fuckin wall to hit at some point.
So everybody will maintain serious face and keep bullshitting until it all goes utterly to shit.

* According to the Bank of Canada, the annual inflation rate in Canada has been a steady 2% since 1991. Igor has some problems with the central bank's accounting methods.

Like people of my calibre are being fuckin destroyed.
Like what's the problem if I'm doing with scrap what city cannot do? Meanwhile we're sinking every day deeper and deeper in city debts?
They just keep wrenching, keep trying to kill this initiative.
3000 bucks, your typical owner in Toronto pays in land tax. Not enough. They should fuckin rake it up, man.
You don't have the money, well then fuckin rent out part of your fuckin shithole, right?
Who says you have to have 800 square feet for your fat ass, right?
The way this is managed is fuckin beyond... it's beyond the description of English language.

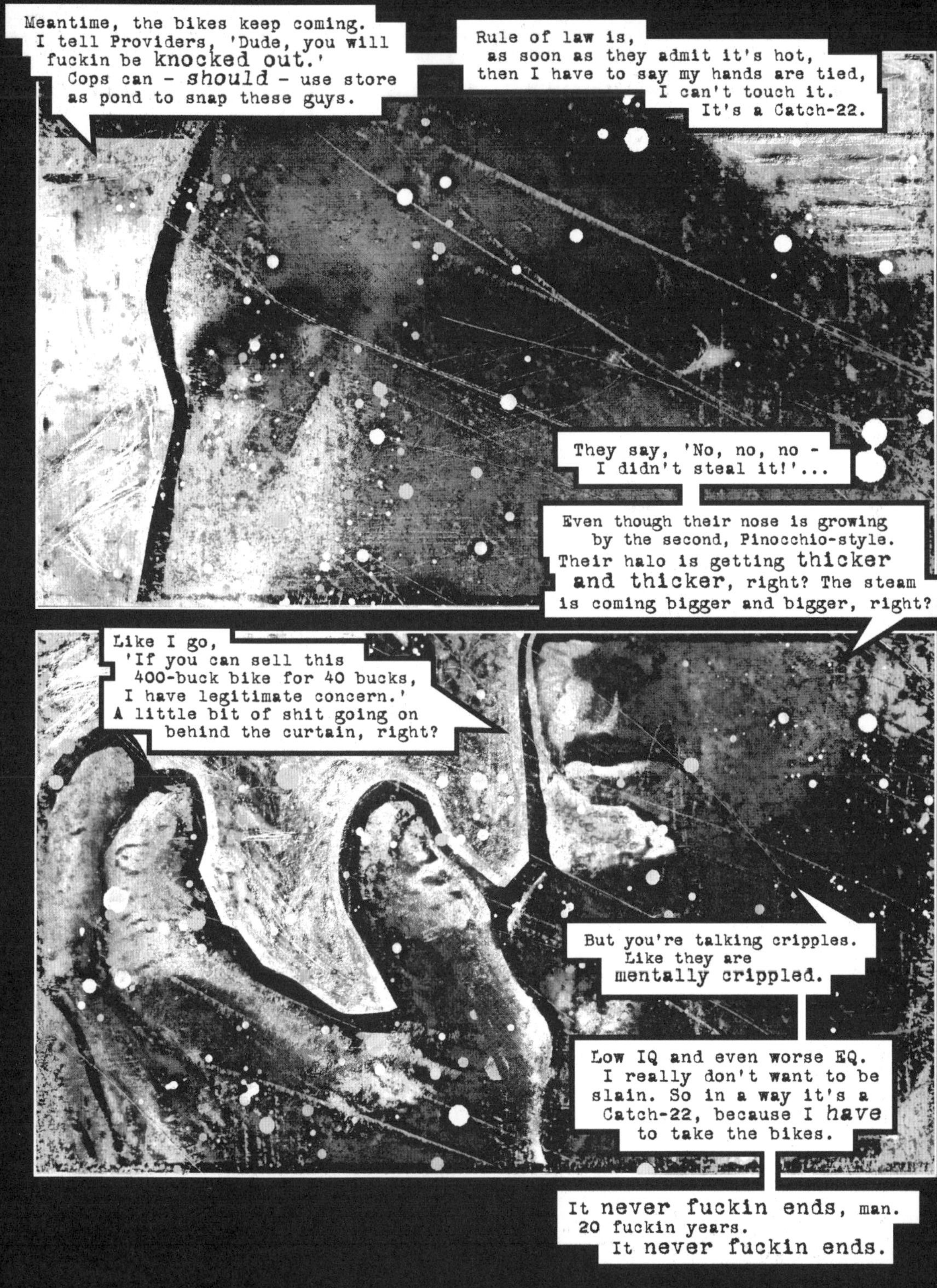
Meantime, the bikes keep coming. I tell Providers, 'Dude, you will fuckin be knocked out.' Cops can - should - use store as pond to snap these guys.
Rule of law is, as soon as they admit it's hot, then I have to say my hands are tied, I can't touch it. It's a Catch-22.
They say, 'No, no, no - I didn't steal it!'...
Even though their nose is growing by the second, Pinocchio-style. Their halo is getting thicker and thicker, right? The steam is coming bigger and bigger, right?
Like I go, 'If you can sell this 400-buck bike for 40 bucks, I have legitimate concern.' A little bit of shit going on behind the curtain, right?
But you're talking cripples. Like they are mentally crippled.
Low IQ and even worse EQ. I really don't want to be slain. So in a way it's a Catch-22, because I have to take the bikes.
It never fuckin ends, man. 20 fuckin years. It never fuckin ends.

I cannot get free from these guys. Even though on paper, I'm almost millionaire. I could retire. But that's punnishment. Even if they give me 10 million under condition that I'm not allowed to work, I wouldn't sign for that treat.
No.
I can only exist to spring out of bed and to be in fuckin panic. To sip on fuckin coffee and run through the fuckin door. Hustle until I feel like I'm barely standing, coming home and fuckin falling in shower and scrub and scrub half a pound of shit off of me.

Photos by Tony Cerbini and Jonathan Ng

I've just come back from fuckin Bahamas. Tanned, 10 pounds fatter and 2000 bucks poorer. My chick wanted to go. But it was Caribbean jail. Murder.
The goal is maintaining Monkey Factor. That's the final goal. Stay alive and keep smiling. According to my calculus - you can only be happy if you're struggling.
However - struggling because YOU want to. Not because anybody else wants you to.

But on paper, I'm fuckin imbecile, right?
All day, every day - I'm looking to get busted, right?
It's great - I didn't get busted today.
Guaranteed Monkey Factor.

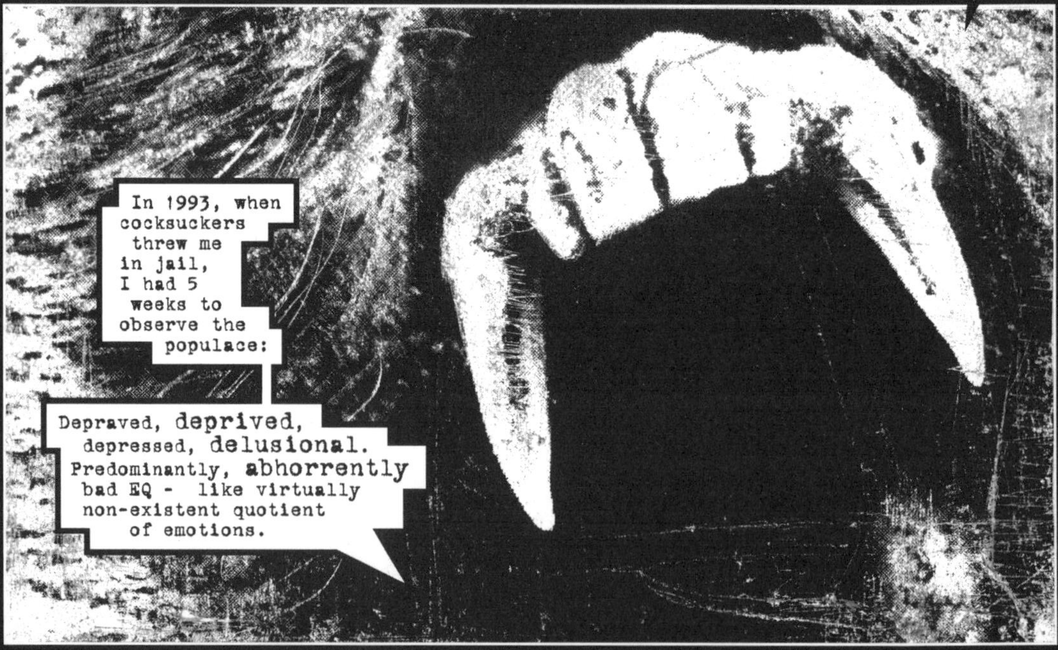
In 1993, when cocksuckers threw me in jail, I had 5 weeks to observe the populace:
Depraved, deprived, depressed, delusional. Predominantly, abhorrently bad EQ - like virtually non-existent quotient of emotions.

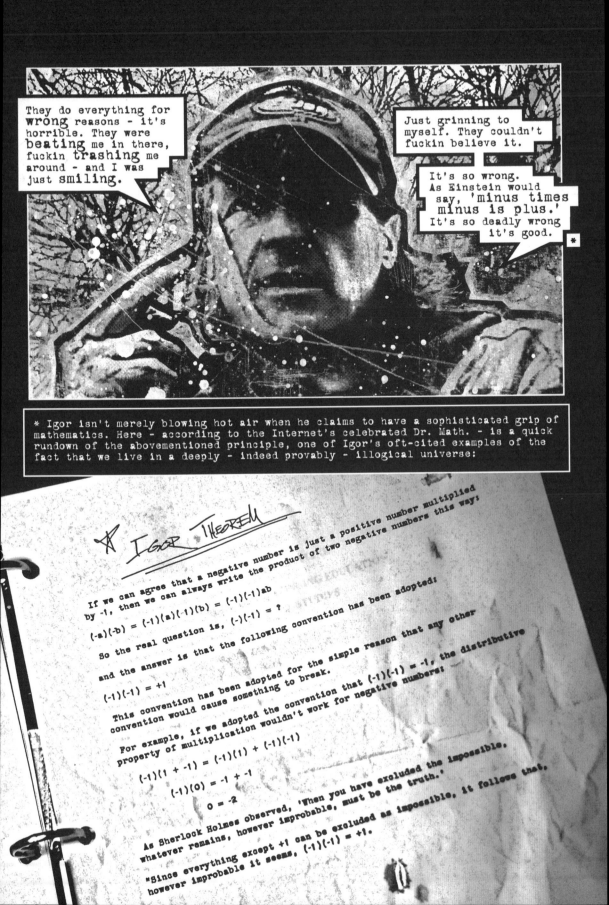

They do everything for wrong reasons - it's horrible. They were beating me in there, fuckin trashing me around - and I was just smiling.
Just grinning to myself. They couldn't fuckin believe it.
It's so wrong. As Einstein would say, 'minus times minus is plus.' It's so deadly wrong it's good.
*

* Igor isn't merely blowing hot air when he claims to have a sophisticated grip of mathematics. Here - according to the Internet's celebrated Dr. Math. - is a quick rundown of the abovementioned principle, one of Igor's oft-cited examples of the fact that we live in a deeply - indeed provably - illogical universe:

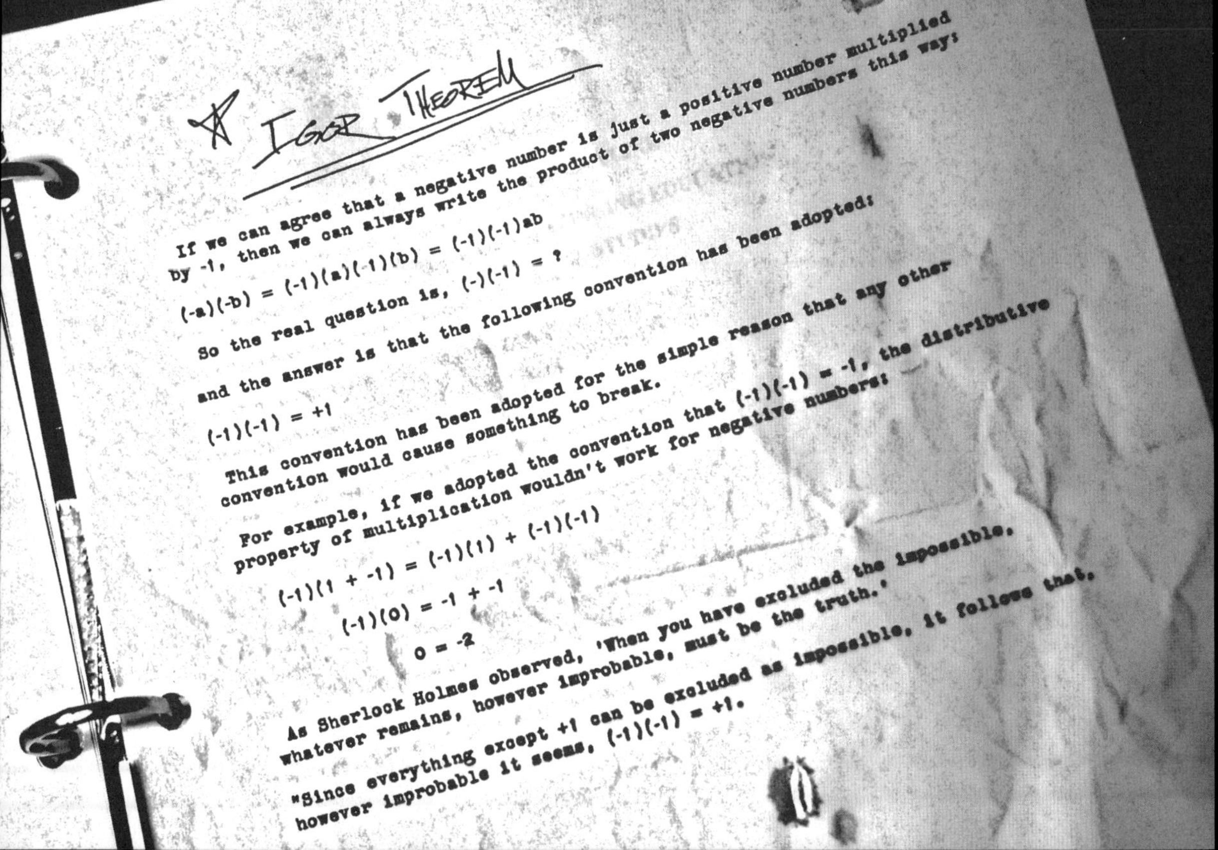

★ IGOR THEOREM

If we can agree that a negative number is just a positive number multiplied by -1, then we can always write the product of two negative numbers this way:

(-a)(-b) = (-1)(a)(-1)(b) = (-1)(-1)ab

So the real question is, (-)(-1) = ?

and the answer is that the following convention has been adopted:

(-1)(-1) = +1

This convention has been adopted for the simple reason that any other convention would cause something to break.

For example, if we adopted the convention that (-1)(-1) = -1, the distributive property of multiplication wouldn't work for negative numbers:

(-1)(1 + -1) = (-1)(1) + (-1)(-1)

(-1)(0) = -1 + -1

0 = -2

As Sherlock Holmes observed, 'When you have excluded the impossible, whatever remains, however improbable, must be the truth.'

"Since everything except +1 can be excluded as impossible, it follows that, however improbable it seems, (-1)(-1) = +1.

Look at this place now.
Big money, right?
Fancy neighbourhood.
Ha! People are still struggling here. They're just pretending.
This is lies and deceptions.
That was one of the topics of my writing.
Lies and deceptions.
It's hurting me that it doesn't matter whether you're telling truth or lies - it's just hollow.
People are hollow.
Non-existing.
There is nothing there.
I don't belong here.
There's no Monkey Factor anymore.
So, I am looking to east of Moss Park for new shop.
But it would be bloodshed.
I fear for being killed in fact, if I open in the east end...
Because there's rows and rows of 'bike shops.'
What's being sold out of there?
Coke? Hash?
So it comes like this.
For whatever reason,
I like my underdog status.
I have to be underdog.

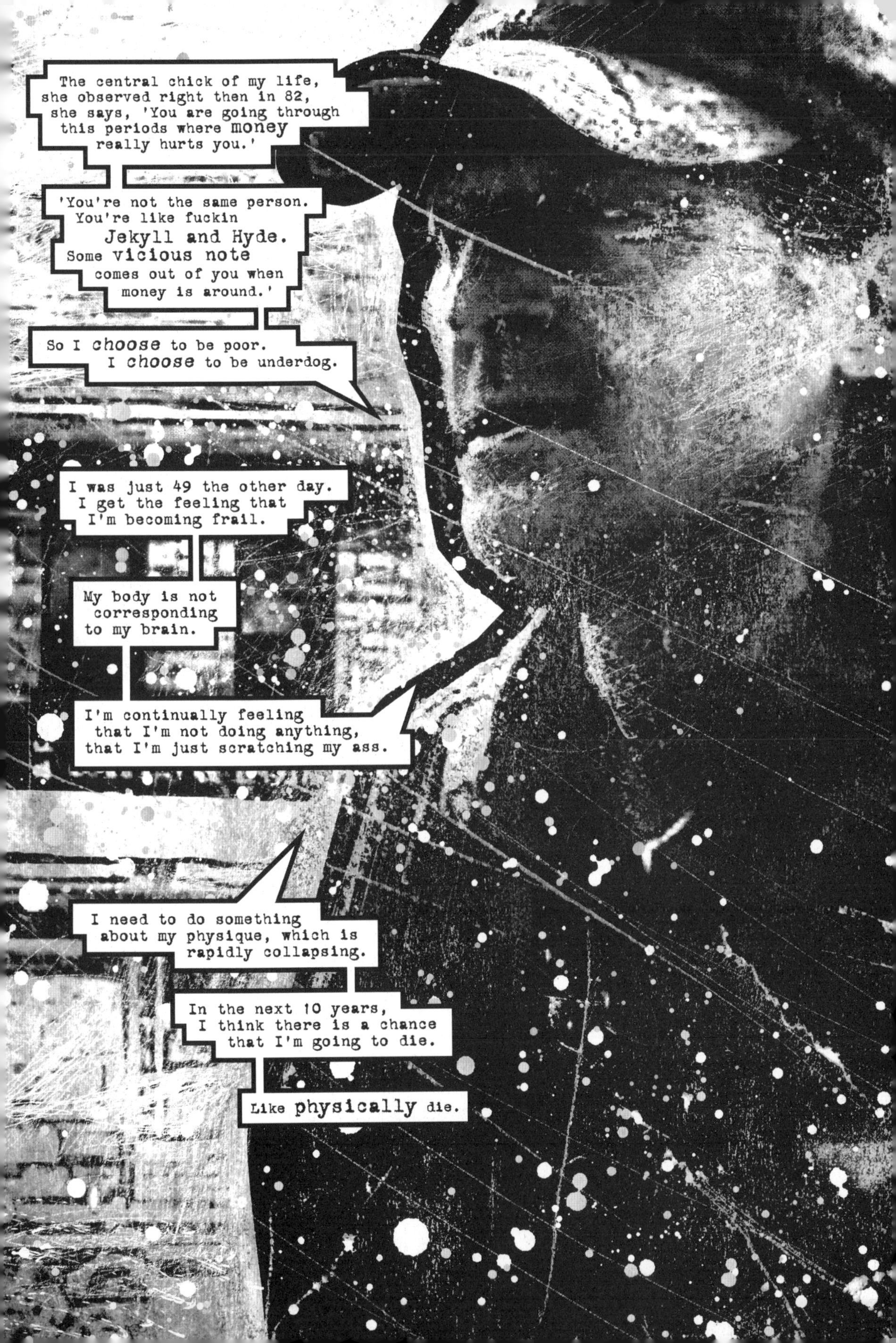
The central chick of my life, she observed right then in 82, she says, 'You are going through this periods where money really hurts you.'
'You're not the same person. You're like fuckin Jekyll and Hyde. Some vicious note comes out of you when money is around.'
So I choose to be poor. I choose to be underdog.
I was just 49 the other day. I get the feeling that I'm becoming frail.
My body is not corresponding to my brain.
I'm continually feeling that I'm not doing anything, that I'm just scratching my ass.
I need to do something about my physique, which is rapidly collapsing.
In the next 10 years, I think there is a chance that I'm going to die.
Like physically die.

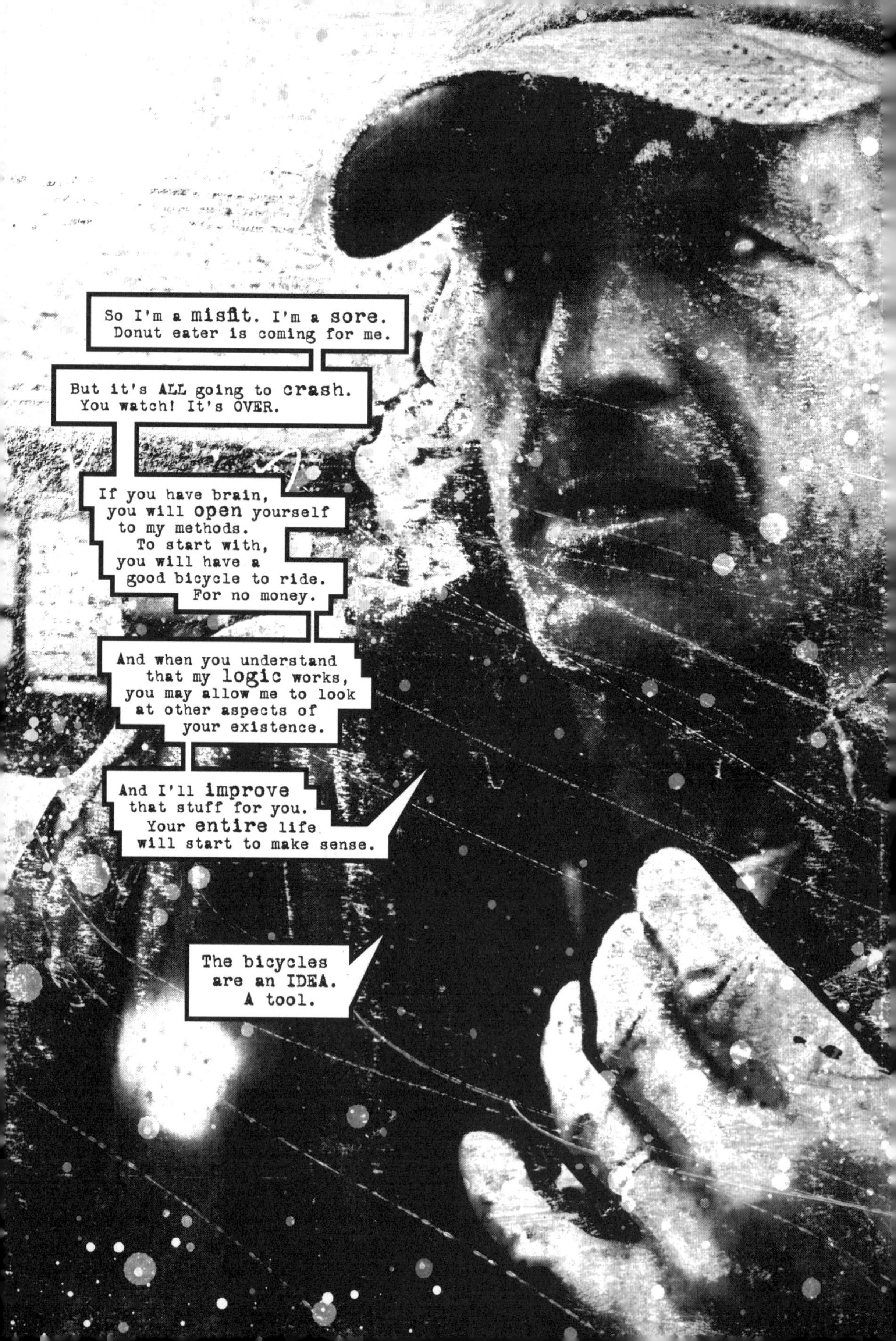
So I'm a misfit. I'm a sore. Donut eater is coming for me.
But it's ALL going to crash. You watch! It's OVER.
If you have brain, you will open yourself to my methods. To start with, you will have a good bicycle to ride. For no money.
And when you understand that my logic works, you may allow me to look at other aspects of your existence.
And I'll improve that stuff for you. Your entire life will start to make sense.
The bicycles are an IDEA. A tool.

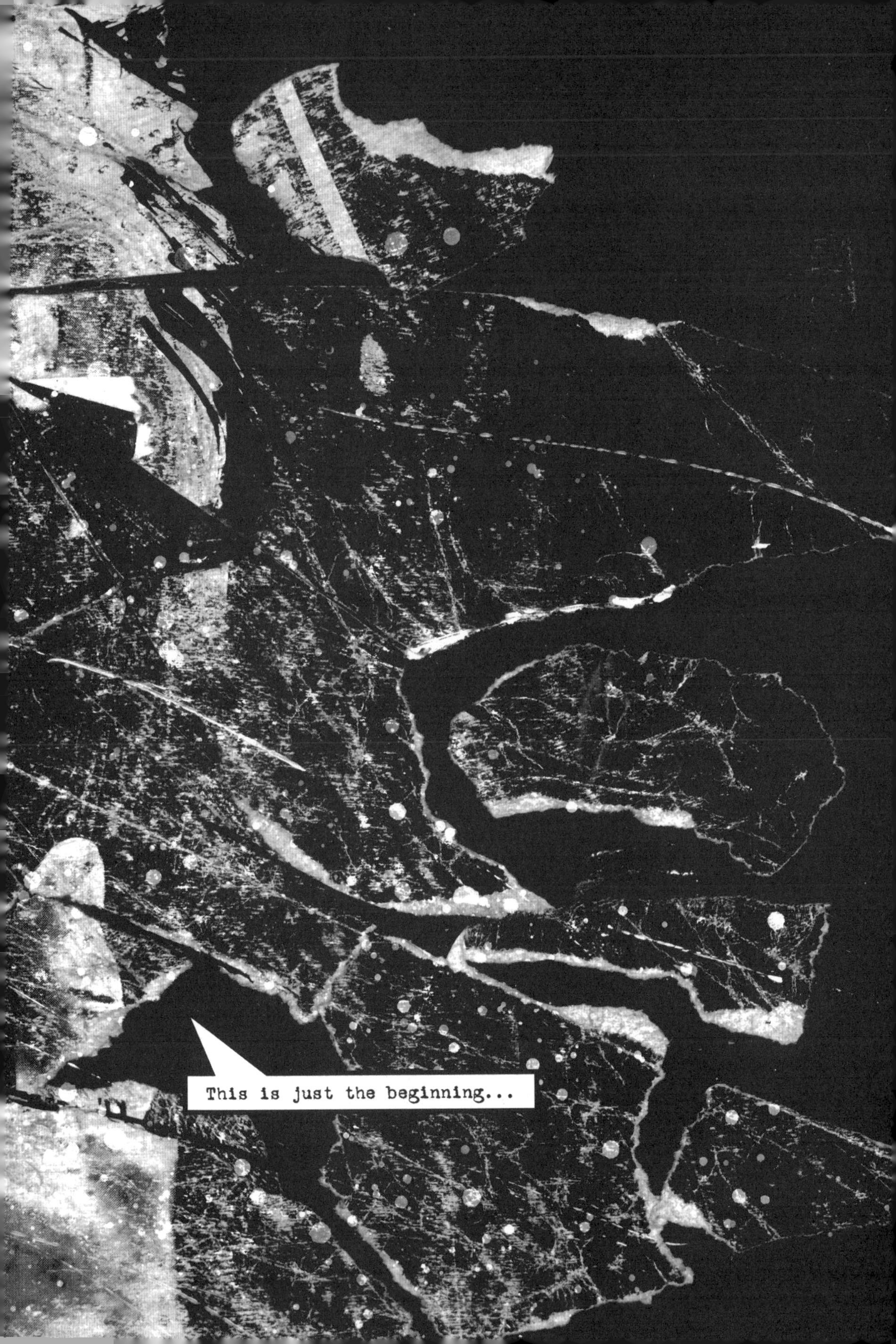
This is just the beginning...

Trinity Bellwoods Park, 1913

Photo courtesy of the City of Toronto Archives

We will return
to the time of
Monkey Factor.
And then you
will listen.
Then
you will need
my methods.

Summer 2008

RECOMM
ADULT ENT
PARKING
ONLY
ALL OTHERS WILL BE COMPACTED
WONDER
GASOLINE
PARKING
ONLY
ALL OTHERS WILL BE TOWED
EX-LAX
Coca-Cola
GUIDANCE ROOM
SPITTING
TOILET
OUT OF ORDER
Please Use -
Far Corner
PRICES
SUBJECT TO CHANGE
ACCORDING TO
CUSTOMER'S
ATTITUDE

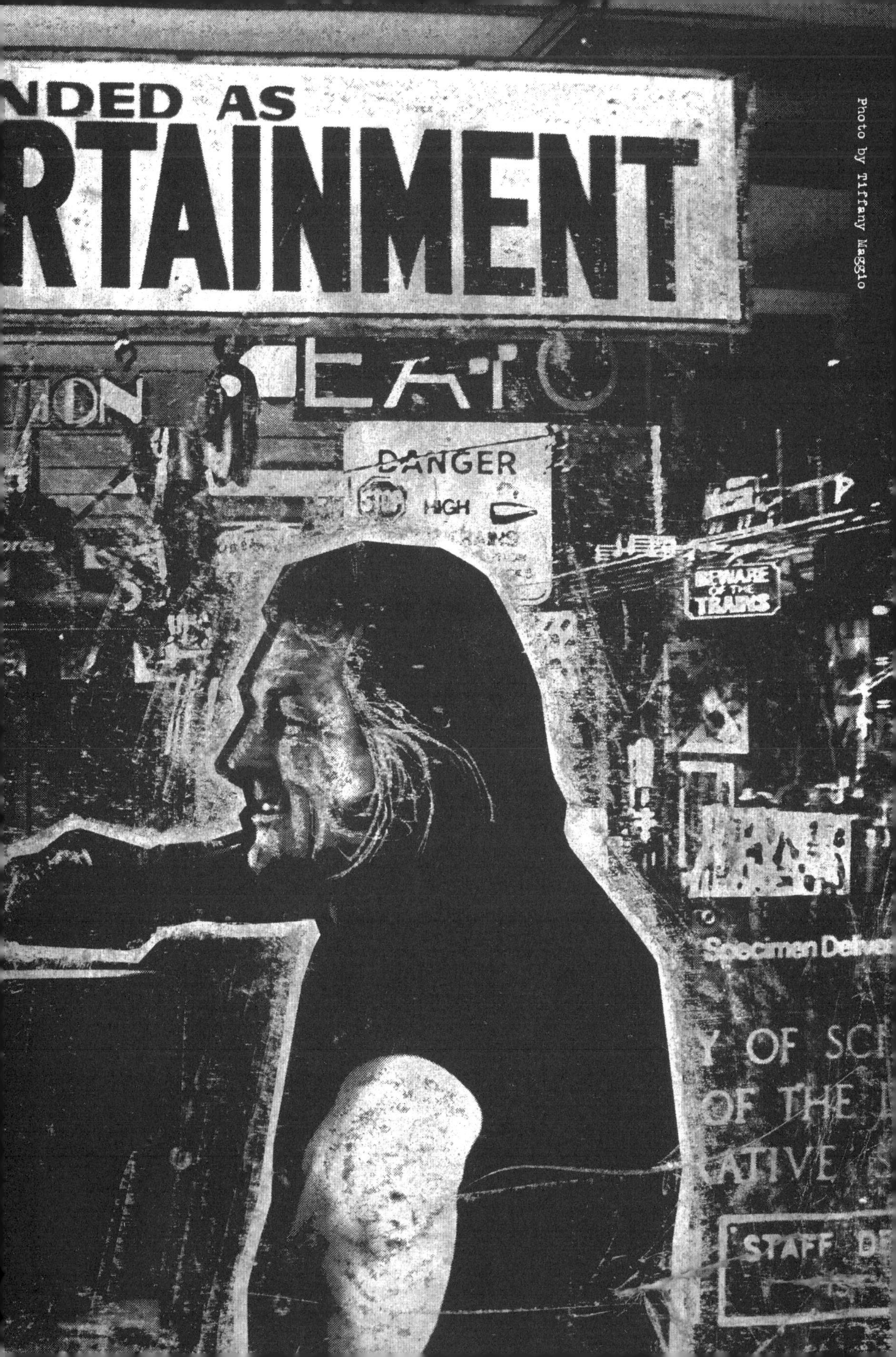
NDED AS
RTAINMENT
DANGER
HIGH
BEWARE OF THE TRAINS
Specimen Delive
Y OF SC
OF THE
ATIVE
STAFF DE

Photo by Tiffany Maggio

GPS Interlude

In September 2006, the University of Toronto - a massive institution with its own community police force - acknowledged that bikes were being stolen from campus with astonishing frequency. Locking a bike up anywhere near the school meant that it would likely go missing.

The university's police decided on a radical solution: They would use bicycles baited with GPS tracking devices to track down the thieves. They seeded the campus with several such bikes, and saw encouraging results.

When this came to the attention of 14 Division's planner, Robert Tajti, he scoured the data and realized that he could back up the community's longstanding claim that no bike was - or ever had been - safe in the Queen West neighbourhood. So, he borrowed the pilot program.

The first thing 14 Division needed was bait bikes. And there was only one logical place to go for such a resource.

Armed with several choice items from Igor's stock, the program was scheduled for summer 2008.

IM TIRED
IM TIRED
IM TIRED
And Your Highness's name is...?
IM TIRED
And do we know our social insurance number by heart?
Whoa, that's a huge frame, man.
It's gonna be lovely job finding forks for that.
fork it over! ha ha!
A comedian...

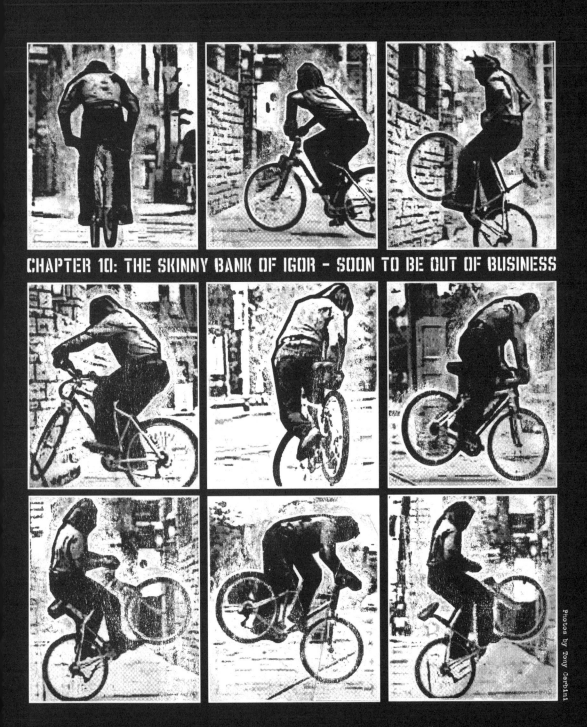

CHAPTER 10: THE SKINNY BANK OF IGOR - SOON TO BE OUT OF BUSINESS

Photos by Tony Cerbini

Photo by Tony Gerbini

...Yeah, but what you gonna put as collateral?
Oh? You have some on you?
Okay, so then we can do the 100 bucks.
No - wait - what? You don't have anything on you? That's not good.
Yeah, sure. Everybody's good for it. But I get fuckin smoked all the time.
Why don't you just grab something and have me hold it for you?
Yeah - ideally I'm not throwing money at people anymore. Because way too many people are not returning my money.
I know, I know. Everybody says, 'Not me!' But I'm giving away my money. That's not business.
So try to get something that I can hold against, right?

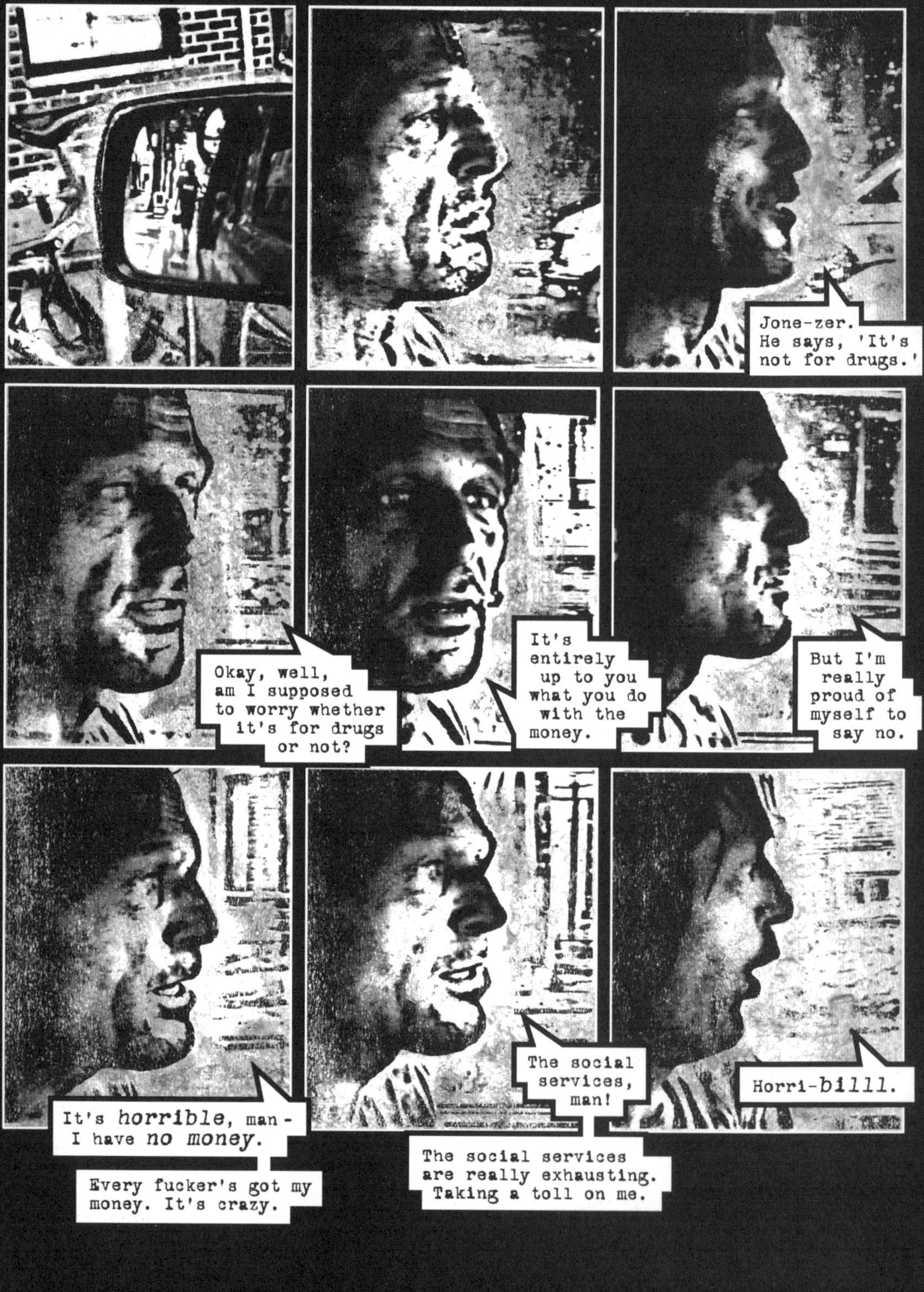
Jone-zer.
He says, 'It's not for drugs.'
Okay, well, am I supposed to worry whether it's for drugs or not?
It's entirely up to you what you do with the money.
But I'm really proud of myself to say no.
It's *horrible*, man - I have *no money*.
Every fucker's got my money. It's crazy.
The social services, man!
The social services are really exhausting. Taking a toll on me.
Horri-*billl*.

And then I have to harass my bunny to lend me her money.
Is that shit or what?
I keep calling everyone LOSER and I come crying.
Huh! Huh! Huh! Huh! Huh! - help me!
I mean, now I'm behaving the same as my losers that say, 'Oh Igor - knock knock knock - I need some money.'
The Bank of Igor. The skinny Bank of Igor.
Soon to be out of business.

In subjective terms, of course, like in Monkey Factor terms - this is good that I'm giving away my money.
This is like a fuckin communism.
But the thing is...
...these people don't deserve any help, really.
So partially I give them the money because it reduces the chance that they go right now and fuck somebody up.
The Bank of Igor. Fuck....
But, you know, we must face it.
I am outrageous. I do like my bending of law, right?
In my opinion, I don't really do anything that deserves to be crucified.
But let's face it - I am troublemaker.

Oh!
I been eyeing that bike for days...
Adelaide Street West, Toronto's Entertainment District

Bike thefts 'really

More than 50,000 have been reported stolen since 1997 – 4,600 last year alone

BRETT CLARKSON
Sun Media

It's 3 a.m. on a Sunday and Steven MacLeod is done his shift at the Big Bop, a Queen and Bathurst Sts. dive that caters mainly to the punk crowd.

He expects to find his bike nearby on the street where he left it locked up.

Thieves, however, would have other plans.

"The only thing left was the U-lock on the ground with a two-by-four," MacLeod says. "They actually used a two-by-four to wrench the U-lock off my bike."

Despite the late hour, the intersection is still teeming with a motley mix of Goth and punk kids, well-dressed clubbers, and the usual cast of drunken characters camped out on the steps of the old bank building on the northwest corner.

MacLeod, a 37-year-old doorman/sound guy, can't believe his $400 bike was ripped off in full view of the busy intersection on a Saturday night.

"Unfortunately, we live in a city where people turn a blind eye to bike theft. It's pathetic," McLeod says.

It's a frustrating scene all too familiar for the tens of thousands of cyclists who have had their bikes stolen in Toronto over the past 10 years.

"I would say bike theft in Toronto is a really big problem," says Dave Hoyle, a mechanic at the Community Bicycle Network on Queen St. W. "I think that's fairly obvious to everyone. I don't think I'm going out on a limb by saying that, because there's just so many people who have had their bikes stolen.

"It just happens all the time."

According to Toronto Police, more than 50,000 bikes have been reported stolen in the city since 1997. Last year alone, 4,585 bicycles were reported stolen in Toronto.

Not even close

But everyone, including police, cycling advocates and average cyclists on the street, believe those numbers are nowhere near accurate because most people don't bother to report their stolen bike.

"The percentage of stolen bikes that are reported to police is not even close to the actual number of bike thefts," says Staff-Sgt. Laurie Jackson of the Community Response Unit of 14 Division, the west-end division that saw the most reported stolen bikes in the city last year, with 589.

Jackson is so blunt because she — along with pretty much the entire Toronto Police Service — wants to see more cyclists registering their bikes on the Toronto Police Bike Registry Database, which has so far logged 50,000 bikes.

IGOR KENK
Owner of the Bicycle Clinic

Sean Wheldrake, the city's bicycle promotions coordinator, estimates the real number is closer to about 12,000 stolen bikes a year.

But Wheldrake also adds that while the number is cause for concern, it's relatively low compared to the number of cyclists in the city.

"Here in Toronto we have 2.6 million people and probably a million cyclists, yet we're having 10,000 or 12,000 bikes stolen a year, so I wouldn't call it a big problem," Wheldrake says, adding that the oft-repeated mantra that Toronto is the bike-theft capital of North America simply isn't true.

According to bike-lock maker Kryptonite, Toronto isn't even in the Top 10 worst cities for bike theft, a list that includes Philadelphia, Chicago, and New York in the Top 3.

"It's totally unfounded," Wheldrake says. "Bike theft is directly related to property theft, so there's obviously a lot of U.S. cities that have a lot more (bicycle) theft than we do."

But still, nobody with even a passing interest in cycling denies that bicycle theft is a pervasive problem here.

So just where do all the stolen bikes go?

Igor Kenk stands amid the mountain of hundreds of bicycles piled up in the backyard behind his Queen St. W. store.

If you listen to the word on the street, this is where stolen bikes go to die.

"Clearly I'm the most infamous loser in this city as far as bike theft goes," says a sarcastic Kenk, who squirts oil from a dirty plastic squeeze bottle on to some of the bikes. A shred of tissue paper that doubles as a bandage is stuck to a bloody cut on his blackened, greasy forearm.

Kenk, 49, owns Bicycle Clinic — though there's no sign on the store — at 927 Queen St. W. For years, the Slovenian bike mechanic has been a fixture on the sidewalk outside his shop across from Trinity Bellwoods Park, with his long stringy hair, hip pack, and the tools he uses to fix up or "recycle" old bikes.

"I am devoted to bikes. Bikes are the best machine, the best invention ever," says Kenk, who opened up his first store in 1992 at 986 Queen St. W. before moving to his current address in 1995 after buying the building for $85,000.

Recently, he's been offered as much as $600,000 for the property, a price tag he's turned down.

"What am I going to do with all that money? Stick it up my a--?"

Judo-trained and admittedly "out there," Kenk knows full well that since the early 1990s he's been suspected of being the go-to guy for thieves hoping to unload stolen bikes for $50 a pop.

In fact, mention bike theft to anybody who has any interest in cycling, whether it be bike shop staffers, cycling advocates, city licensing officials, the cops who arrest the thieves, or even just the average-Joe cyclist, and Kenk's name is mentioned — without fail.

"I'm a thief, I'm the darkest nightmare in the western hemisphere," says Kenk, again sarcastically, poking fun at his own dubious reputation.

The truth is — and Kenk acknowledges this — some of the bikes piled up in his backyard and in his store are most likely stolen. Some, not all. The same thing would be true for every pawn shop in the city, he says.

But according to both Kenk and Richard Mucha, the city's manager of licensing, Kenk is operating legally and doing everything by the book.

Kenk keeps the city-issued registry book — second-hand shop owners must fill it in every time somebody sells them a used item — near the door of his shop when he's working, and says he always asks for two pieces of ID from would-be sellers. Any information about the bike, including its serial number and physical description, is logged, along with the seller's information. The information is relayed to police frequently, Kenk says.

"Bikes that have been floating around the market end up here, and end up in the (registry) book," Kenk says. "They (the police) get the ledgers, they get what they want."

And still, the thieves roll up on bikes to his shop. It's a Monday night and a clean-cut young man wearing a baseball cap pulls up on a mountain bike.

"This guy got pinched al[...] I'm not going to buy from hi[...]" says quietly to a reporter [...] walking over to inspect the b[...]

Within moments, the ma[...]ing off down Queen St. W., [...] to another pawn shop.

"He got pinched so now [...] (sell to me). It's a piece of sh[...]" says about the bike the appar[...] was trying to flog. "I don't li[...] new wave, disposable $99 bi[...]"

Back outside, Kenk menti[...] the occasional angry theft vic[...]

SUN

SAVING T.O.

An ongoing series on fixing the decline of our great city

Toronto isn't ranked in the Top 10 cities for bicycle thievery in North America but tell that to Steven MacLeod who had his $400 bike pin[...]

SUNDAY SUN NEWS JULY 13, 2008

'big problem'

come by the store hoping to find their bike, including a raging man who attacked him recently and was rewarded with a punch in the head for his aggressiveness.

Theft victims will occasionally find their bikes at Kenk's shop, and he said if they can prove he has their bike, he'll give it back to them.

Kenk agrees the current system may be too lax and despite the fact stolen bikes find their way to his store, he says bike theft needs to be addressed somehow.

"Nobody's willing to work on the issue. They just know that I'm the 'bandit' and that's that. I don't give a sh--," Kenk says. "My job is to put (the stolen bike) in police hands, and I challenge anybody that's barking — I challenge them. Let's go to work. I agree, it's a mess. It's a mess, all this sh-- floating around."

Have a story about a stolen bike? Contact reporter Brett Clarkson at brett.clarkson@sunmedia.ca

KRYPTONITE
STUCKS LOCK

Mark Duke, sales manager at Duke's Cycle on Richmond St. W., s

...ways to safeguard y...

Toronto newspapers have a long tradition of publishing "we're the bike theft capital of the world" articles, and on July 13, a *Toronto Sun* reporter named Brett Clarkson filed just such a piece, in which Igor was quoted as saying, "I'm a thief, I'm the darkest nightmare in the western hemisphere," while insisting that the cops were utterly useless in battling bike theft.

The article caused the usual community consternation, and a day or so after it ran, Clarkson got a call from 14 Division planner Robert Tajti, asking him to do a ride-along to see exactly what the police were doing about the problem.

The ride-along was scheduled for the morning of July 16.

That morning, perhaps inspired by all the chatter from the *Toronto Sun* article, Igor invited a local photographer to take some staged photographs parodying his reputation as the 'biggest thief in western hemisphere.'

Photo by Tiffany Maggio

Mission
resolutely
accomplished

Photo by Tiffany Maggio

Some hours later, Brett Clarkson of the *Toronto Sun* found himself in a squad car trawling the Queen Street West 'hood, staking out the baited bikes. The car was parked at the northern end of Trinity Bellwoods Park when an excited call squawked through. The officer in charge explained that a local bike-shop owner had just been observed ordering an associate to cut a bike lock with bolt cutters, after which he paid for the bicycle with cash. Two men stood in handcuffs just outside Igor's Bicycle Clinic.

Clarkson has said that he knew then that he was reporting on the end of an era.

Igor is pushed into a squad car by a plainclothes policeman, July 16, 2008

DO NOT
ENTER

Center for
Poor Karma & Pain
Research

Photo by Francis Mariani

4053
Findlay
BATES & DODDS FUNERA
CLAFOUTI

CLAFOUTI
WHERE'S
IGOR
?

DO NOT
ENTER

IGOR
DO NOT ENTER

EPILOGUE

Igor's Bicycle Clinic, November 2009 - 16 months after major bust

HELP!
FREE
STUFF
Enter at
Your Own Risk

Author's Summary

On July 16, 2008, Igor Kenk was arrested outside his store and charged with 2 counts of possession of stolen property. 2 days later, following a tip that Kenk paid for bikes with cash and drugs, a justice of the peace issued search warrants for 12 premises dotted over the Toronto area. The police recovered 2,865 bicycles, innumerable bike parts, and a $15,000 sculpture called the Centaur. In the residence Kenk shared with his common-law wife Jeanie Chung, a comprehensive search turned up 56 grams of cocaine and 8 kgs of marijuana, along with at least $3,000 in cash.

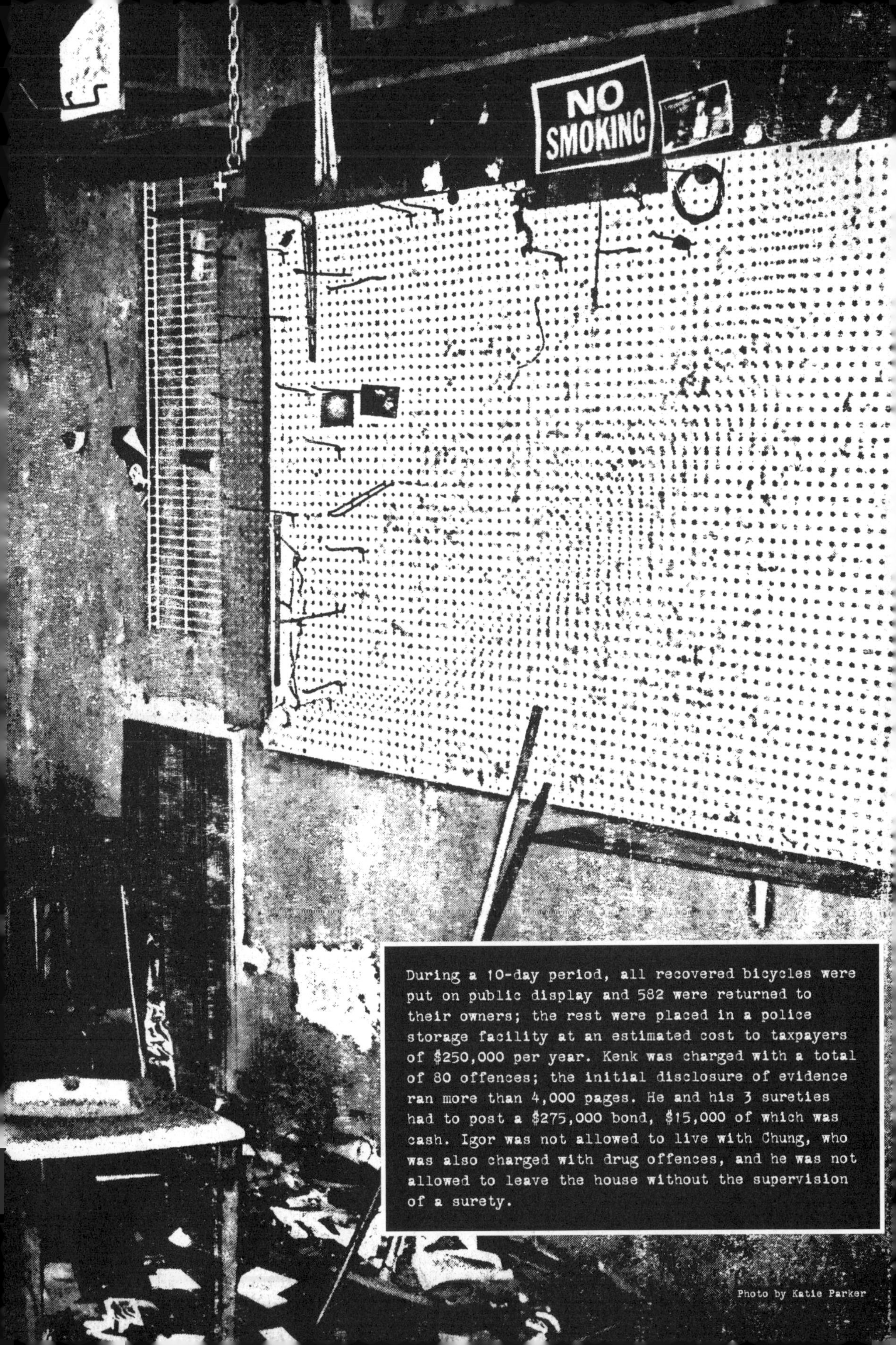
NO
SMOKING

During a 10-day period, all recovered bicycles were put on public display and 582 were returned to their owners; the rest were placed in a police storage facility at an estimated cost to taxpayers of $250,000 per year. Kenk was charged with a total of 80 offences; the initial disclosure of evidence ran more than 4,000 pages. He and his 3 sureties had to post a $275,000 bond, $15,000 of which was cash. Igor was not allowed to live with Chung, who was also charged with drug offences, and he was not allowed to leave the house without the supervision of a surety.

Photo by Katie Parker

Igor's remaining stock - 2,300 bicycles and 1,000s of wheels and other miscellany - stored in a disused school owned by 14 Division

On December 14, 2008, while visiting one of his rental units, Kenk is alleged to have had an altercation with a Pakistani family that had very recently moved into the home, during which he reportedly swung a metal pipe at a pregnant woman. He was arrested, charged with assault and 3 days later his bail was revoked. These charges have since been stayed.

He was remanded to Toronto's Don Jail, where he claimed that he was severely beaten by fellow inmates. His lawyer, Lon Rose, made repeated requests for medical clemency, all of which were denied. Perhaps because of the scale of the Crown's case, Rose maintained that the Crown and the police were consistently tardy in providing disclosures. Kenk made dozens of court appearances over the course of 2009, none of which were conclusive.

Local and international media continued to cover the story, and Torontonians continued to be outraged. Numerous conspiracy theories were touted: that Kenk was part of the Russian mafia and planned to send bicycles back to Eastern Europe in shipping containers; that the cops he had for so long conspired with sold him out; that area developers colluded on pushing him out when he refused to sell his shop. Jeanie Chung had to forfeit her passport and could not travel for work. Following his initial cleanup for his bail hearing in 2008, Kenk began appearing in court in an increasingly dishevelled state, with long hair and a shaggy beard.

Under threat of the Civil Remedies Act - in which the Crown can seize property they deem likely to have been involved in criminal activity - Kenk agreed to sell his 927 Queen Street West property, his 2 trucks and the 1,000s of bikes in police storage. His storefront was purchased for a reported $640,000, $50,000 of which went to the province and an unspecified portion to cover all legal fees. Any remaining proceeds are Kenk's. Meanwhile his remaining possessions were placed outside the shop and given away for free.

In December 2009, after lengthy negotiations between Lon Rose and the Crown, Kenk pleaded guilty to 10 counts of bicycle theft and 6 drug charges. The Crown attorney noted that the plea would significantly reduce the costs of what was becoming an increasingly expensive legal procedure. Kenk was sentenced to 30 months in jail, with the justice of the peace counting the 13 months he served in the Don Jail as time +1. All charges against Jeanie Chung were dropped.

On March 5, 2010,
after nearly 15 months behind bars,
Igor Kenk walked from the Don Jail
a free man.

Photo by Laura Jane Patelko
March 5, 2010

END

Produced and Conceived by Alex Jansen

Written by Richard Poplak

Filmed and Designed by Jason Gilmore

Illustrated by Nick Marinkovich

Original Source Footage
Directed by:
Jason Gilmore and Alex Jansen
Filmed by: Jason Gilmore
Interviews by: Alex Jansen

Supplementary Footage by:
Anthony Corindia
Tiffany Maggio
Richard Poplak

Source Photography:
Jason Gilmore
Tiffany Maggio

Key Additional Photography:
Tanya Canam
Tony Cerbini
Ron Haviv
Alex Jansen
Francis Mariani
Jonathan Ng
Katie Parker
Laura Jane Patelko
Kevin Steele
Haim Vaginshtein
Steven Wasney
*Additional source material
credited in following section

Clearance:
Alex Jansen
Clearance Consultant:
Tanya Fleet
Clearance Assistance:
Brendan Hennessy

Legal Review:
Bob Tarantino, Heenan Blaikie LLP
Additional Legal Assistance:
Tony Duarte

Art Direction:
Richard Poplak and Jason Gilmore
Layout & Design: Jason Gilmore

Edited by:
Alex Jansen

Substantive Editor,
Copy Editor & Fact Checker:
Lorna Poplak
Transcription:
Katie Parker with
Simone Rodrigue
Proofreaders:
Katie Parker
Lorna Poplak
Medeine Tribinevicius

Production and
Research Assistance:
Sarah-Joyce Battersby
Amita Bhatia
Alex Chechik
Jenny Cooper
Brendan Hennessy
Alexis Mitchell
Craig Jackson
Katie Parker

Marketing & Publicity:
Alex Jansen
Canadian Publicist:
Dan Wagstaff, Raincoast Books
Canadian Publicity Consultant:
Stephen Meyers
Special Events Coordinator:
Jenny Cooper
Web Sales & Marketing Coordinator:
Brendan Hennessy
Web Sales & Marketing Administrator:
Sean Cartwright

Trailer Animation:
Craig Small

Interactive On-Line Preview
Directed by:
Shahid Quadri
Programmed by:
zegap
Produced with the Support of
The CFC Media Lab

Web Designer:
Jason Gilmore
Web Programmer:
Andrea Acosta Duarte
Web Master:
Brendan Hennessy

IT Support:
Conrad Spunde

Distributed in Canada by:
Raincoast Books

Special Thanks:

Madalena Xanthopoulos
Mark Achbar
Hussain Amarshi & Mongrel Media
Cathy Barrett
Darlene Barrowman
Sumit Bhatia
Janet Bike Girl & CineCycle
Peter Birkmoe & The Beguiling
Shaun Bradley
Chris Butcher & TCAF
Anka Cheburashka Dmitrovic
Sarah Cooper
Chad Cranston
Leanne Fogarty
Anthea Foyer
Andrew Frank
Sarah Fulford
Marc Glassman
Richard Goddard
Christine Haebler
Chandra Halko
Ron Haviv
Harry & Sylvie Jansen
Eric Kamphof & Curbside Cycle
Lia Kyranis
Paddy Laidley & Raincoast Books

Carey Low
Clarke Mackey
Lea Marin
Hui-an Marinkovich
Zoey Marinkovich - Nightgarden Seminar Co-ordinator
Melanie McLaren
Michael Nicholson
Mike Noonan
Lindsay Page
Katie Parker
Nick de Pencier
Simone Rodrigue
Ana Serano & the CFC Media Lab
Seth
Craig Small & The Juggernaut
Russell Smith
Conrad Spunde
Chris Staros
Bob Tarantino
Charles Tremblay
Duncan Vignale
Dan Wannemacher
Tim Willison, Camas Winsor & Oddly Studios
Matt Youmans

Additional Copyright Source Material Credits:

Back Cover: Original photograph by Tiffany Maggio

Epigraph: Original photograph by Tony Cerbini

Page 2, panel 4: Material reprinted with the express permission of: "The National Post Company," a Canwest Partnership

Page 2, panel 8: Original message board posting, reprinted with the express permission of: "I Bike T.O." (www.ibiketo.ca)

Page 3, panel 3 & 7: Material reprinted with the express permission of: "The National Post Company," a Canwest Partnership

Page 3, panel 8: Original article reprinted with the express permission of: "The Ming Pao Daily News"

Page 3, panel 9 & Page 4, panel 2: Original message board posting, reprinted with the express permission of: "I Bike T.O." (www.ibiketo.ca)

Page 4, panel 6-8: Material reprinted with the express permission of: "Toronto Star," Torstar Syndication Services

Page 5, panel 1: Original message board posting, reprinted with the express permission of: "I Bike T.O." (www.ibiketo.ca)

Page 5, panel 3: Material reprinted with the express permission of: "Toronto Star," Torstar Syndication Services

Page 12, panel 5, 6 & 7, & Page 13: Original photograph by Tony Cerbini

Page 38, panel 1, 3 & 5: Stills from Universal Newsreels, Universal Studios

Page 38, panel 4 & 6, Page 39 & Page 45, panel 2: Original photographs by Ron Haviv

Page 45, panel 7: Original photograph by Haim Vaginshtein

Page 46/47: Original photographs courtesy of Duncan Vignale, Haim Vaginshtein and Tiffany Maggio

Page 61: Original photograph by Steven Wasney

Page 63: Original photograph by Kevin Steele

Page 65: Original photograph by Tiffany Maggio

Page 66-72, panel 1: Stills from original video footage by Anthony Corindia

Page 73: Stills from original video footage by Anthony Corindia

Page 76: Original photograph by Steven Wasney

Page 82 & 107: Original photographs by Tiffany Maggio

Page 179, panel 4: Original photograph by Tanya Canam

Page 209: Original photograph by Jonathan Ng

Page 211, panels 1, 3, 4, 6 & 9, & Pages 220 & 230: Original photographs by Tiffany Maggio

Page 228/29: Original photographs by Tony Cerbini and Jonathan Ng

Page 231, panel 4: Original explanation reprinted with the express permission of: "The Math Forum @ Drexel" (www.mathforum.org)

Page 236/37: Original photograph courtesy of the City of Toronto Archives (series 372, sub-series 52, item 170)

Page 238, panel 1: Original photograph by Madalena Xanthopoulos

Page 238, panels 2, 3, 4 & 9, & Page 240/41: Original photographs by Tiffany Maggio

Page 245/46: Original photographs by Tony Cerbini

Page 254/55: Original article reprinted with the express permission of: "The Toronto Sun," Sun Media Corporation

Page 256/57: Original photographs by Tiffany Maggio

Page 262/63: Original photograph by Francis Mariani

Page 270-273: Original photographs by Katie Parker

Page 283 & Team Photo: Original photographs by Laura Jane Patelko

Jason Gilmore - Alex Jansen - Richard Poplak - Nick Marinkovich

---

Kenk: A Graphic Portrait was conceived as a journalistic comic book by creative producer and publisher Alex Jansen in April 2007. It is built from extensive documentary footage shot by Jansen and filmmaker/designer Jason Gilmore over a 15-month period leading up to Igor Kenk's arrest in July 2008.

Kenk is written by acclaimed journalist Richard Poplak, whose books include *The Sheikh's Batmobile: In Pursuit of American Pop Culture in the Muslim World* and *Ja, No, Man: Growing Up White in Apartheid-Era South Africa* (both published by Penguin).

Working from initial layouts by Jason Gilmore, Toronto-based artist Nick Marinkovich illustrated the pages of *Kenk*. Marinkovich adapted Sony Pictures' *Underworld*, and has worked on various comic book projects with Marvel, IDW and Image.

www.kenk.ca

About Pop Sandbox

Pop Sandbox is a multimedia production and publishing company with a central focus on graphic novels and film. It is a boutique operation centered on innovative and meaningful storytelling across platforms, from initial concept through production to eventual publication/distribution.

Pop Sandbox aims to bring together artists from a variety of backgrounds and disciplines into a creative environment that fosters innovation in both content and form.

www.popsandbox.com